Business Analytics in Practice

The "Business Analytics in Practice" book series highlights the importance of analytics in decision-making across industries and academia. It offers practical insights and case studies for effective implementation of business analytics.

This unique series brings together experts from academia and industry to showcase the latest advancements in decision analytics. It covers a wide range of topics, including AI and Machine Learning, Financial Analytics, Marketing Analytics, Fraud and Risk Analytics, Operations and Supply Chain Analytics, Health Analytics, Human Resources Analytics, Social Media Analytics, Sustainability, and Net-zero Analytics, etc.

Authored by academics and experienced professionals, this book series bridges the gap between academia and industry. Each book combines practical guidance, best practices, and successful case studies, empowering readers to apply analytics to drive business value and explore new data-driven opportunities.

The series emphasizes rigorous research and theoretical foundations while demonstrating the practical impact of decision analytics. In-depth case studies make it an authoritative resource for researchers, academics, practitioners, and students in business analytics, data science, and management science.

Yu Xiong
Editor

Blockchain Analytics for Practitioners

Bridging Theory and Practice

Springer

Editor
Yu Xiong
Surrey Business School
University of Surrey
Guildford, UK

ISSN 2948-2666 ISSN 2948-2674 (electronic)
Business Analytics in Practice
ISBN 978-3-032-06045-7 ISBN 978-3-032-06046-4 (eBook)
https://doi.org/10.1007/978-3-032-06046-4

This Springer imprint is published by the registered company Springer Nature Switzerland AG
The registered company address is: Gewerbestrasse 11, 6330 Cham, Switzerland

About the Editor

Professor Yu Xiong is Chair Professor of Business Analytics in the Surrey Business School at the University of Surrey and a Fellow of the Academy of Social Sciences (FAcSS), recognized for his distinguished contributions to research, innovation, and public policy engagement. A leading expert in blockchain, metaverse, artificial intelligence, and supply chain innovation, Professor Xiong has established himself as a prominent scholar at the intersection of technology and sustainability.

He is the co-founder of Endless Protocol, an AI-embedded Layer One blockchain, and founder of both the Surrey Centre for Innovation and Commercialization and the Surrey Academy for Blockchain and Metaverse Applications (SABMA), where he continues to serve as Director. Professor Xiong has previously held major academic leadership roles, including Associate Vice-President, Associate Dean (International), and Director of Enterprise Engagement, and has served at the Universities of York, Queen's Belfast, East Anglia, and Northumbria. Over his career, he has secured more than £4 million in funding for research, education, and technology commercialization.

Professor Xiong's research focuses on the sustainable and technological transformation of global supply chains, particularly the integration of AI and blockchain to enhance efficiency, transparency, and circular economy outcomes. He has published widely in leading journals such as *Nature Communications, Journal of Operations Management, European Journal of Operational Research, International Journal of Operations and Production Management (IJOPM), Journal of Business Research, International Journal of Production Economics, and The Journal of the Operational Research Society*. He has also served as Guest Editor for *IJOPM, Technovation, and IEEE Transactions Part E.*

He has held distinguished fellowships and visiting appointments, including as a Fellow of the University of Cambridge Institute for Sustainability Leadership (2016–2023), Senior Research Associate at the University of Oxford Technology and Management Centre for Development (2023–present), and Visiting Professor at the Universities of York and Durham.

Beyond academia, Professor Xiong is an active entrepreneur and innovator. He co-founded OxValue.AI, a joint venture with the University of Oxford focused on AI-driven early-stage valuation, which received the Falling Walls Scientific Breakthrough Award (2022) and the Oxford Vice-Chancellor's Award (Highly Commended, 2025). He is also Chair and Co-founder of Keath.AI, recognized as a finalist for both the Times Higher Education Digital University Awards and the PIE News Innovation of the Year Awards (2024). He has advised more than 40 startups and scaleups, including Fotor, a generative AI platform with over 650 million users, and serves as Senior Vice President for Research at Datasection Inc., a Tokyo-listed AI infrastructure company, leading international projects such as the development of next-generation AI data centres.

A passionate advocate for sustainability and responsible innovation, Professor Xiong's work has been featured by the BBC during COP26, and his tourism tokenomics research with Therme Group was showcased at COP28, demonstrating his commitment to aligning technological progress with global sustainability goals.

Chapter 1
Introduction to Blockchain and Its Application

Amit Kumar Jaiswal

1.1 Overview of Blockchain Technology and Its Evolution

Fundamental Cryptographic Primitives in Blockchain Systems
The security and functional integrity of blockchain technologies are deeply rooted in several established cryptographic concepts. This section elaborates on the core primitives including hash functions, hash chains, Merkle trees, and digital signatures, detailing their properties and specific applications within blockchain frameworks.

1.1.1 Cryptographic Hash Functions

A *hash function* denoted as H is formally defined as a deterministic mathematical function that maps an input of arbitrary length, typically a sequence of bits from the set $\{0, 1\}^*$, to a fixed-length output string, often called a *digest* or *hash value*, belonging to $\{0, 1\}^k$ for some fixed integer k (the output size). Mathematically, $H: \{0, 1\}^* \rightarrow \{0, 1\}^k$.

Within the domain of information security, *cryptographic hash functions (CHFs)* are a specialized subset of hash functions engineered to exhibit specific security properties crucial for applications like data integrity verification, digital signatures, and password storage. The indispensable properties of a CHF are:

A. K. Jaiswal (✉)
Endless Protocol, Guildford, UK

University of Surrey, Guildford, UK

Indian Institute of Technology (BHU) Varanasi, Varanasi, India
e-mail: amit@endless.link; a.jaiswal@surrey.ac.uk; amit.chr@iitbhu.ac.in

Y. Xiong (ed.), *Blockchain Analytics for Practitioners*, Business Analytics in Practice, https://doi.org/10.1007/978-3-032-06046-4_1

1. *Computational Efficiency*: For any given input message m, the computation of its digest $H(m)$ must be achievable in polynomial time with respect to the length of m. This ensures practical usability in real-world systems.
2. *Pre-image Resistance (One-Way Property)*: Given a hash value y, it must be computationally infeasible to find *any* input message m such that $H(m) = y$. Computational infeasibility typically implies that no probabilistic polynomial-time (PPT) algorithm can succeed with non-negligible probability. This property prevents an adversary from determining the original input from its hash.
3. *Second Pre-image Resistance (Weak Collision Resistance)*: Given a specific input message m_1, it must be computationally infeasible to find a *different* input message m_2 ($m_2 \neq m_1$) such that $H(m_1) = H(m_2)$. This property protects against targeted forgery where an attacker tries to find an alternative message mapping to the same hash as a known message.

These three properties collectively define what is known as a *One-Way Hash Function (OWHF)* as formalized by Merkle (Rogaway & Shrimpton, 1979). A stronger security notion often required in practice is *Collision Resistance*. A hash function H is deemed collision-resistant if it is computationally infeasible to find any pair of distinct inputs (m_1, m_2), where $m_1 \neq m_2$, such that their digests are identical, i.e. $H(m_1) = H(m_2)$. A function satisfying this additional property is termed a *Collision-Resistant Hash Function (CRHF)*. Collision resistance implies second pre-image resistance (under standard assumptions) but is a fundamentally stronger requirement. Finding collisions is generally easier due to the birthday paradox, which dictates that a collision can likely be found after hashing approximately $2^{k/2}$ inputs for a k-bit hash function, necessitating larger output sizes (e.g., $k = 256$) for adequate security. Hash functions are foundational to blockchain architectures. Different protocols select specific CHFs, for instance, Bitcoin predominantly utilizes SHA-256 (Secure Hash Algorithm 2 with a 256-bit output) belonging to the SHA-2 family which follows the Merkle–Damg°ard construction (Nakamoto, 2008). Ethereum, conversely, employs Keccak-256 which became the SHA-3 standard and is based on the sponge construction, offering different internal mechanisms and security proofs (Buterin, 2013).

1.1.2 Hash Chains

A *hash chain* is constructed through the iterated application of a cryptographic hash function H to an initial value (or secret). Starting with an initial input m_0, a hash chain of length n can be defined as the sequence $h_0, h_1, \ldots, h_n$, where $h_0 = H(m_0)$ and $h_i = H(h_{i-1})$ for $1 \leq i \leq n$. Alternatively, starting from a secret s, one might compute $h_1 = H(s)$, $h_2 = H(h_1)$, ..., $h_n = H(h_{n-1})$. The n-th element can be compactly denoted as $H^n(s)$. Figure 1.1 provides a conceptual illustration. Lamport originally proposed hash chains for secure authentication and password management (Lamport, 1981). In his scheme, a server stores $h_n = H^n(p)$, where p is the user's secret password and

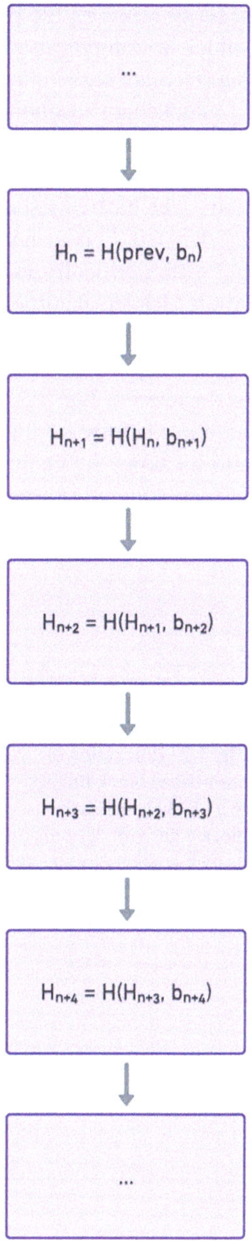

Fig. 1.1 Conceptual representation of a hash chain of length five, derived from an initial message m via iterated hashing with function H

n is a predetermined integer. To authenticate, the user submits $h_{n-1} = H^{n-1}(p)$. The server verifies this by computing $H(h_{n-1})$ and comparing it to the stored h_n. If the values match, authentication is successful, and the server updates its stored value to h_{n-1} for the next session. This process continues iteratively (h_{n-2}, h_{n-3}, …). The security relies on the pre-image resistance of H, ensuring that eavesdropped hash values or compromised server storage does not reveal the original password p or intermediate hash values closer to p.

Blockchain technology employs a related concept to establish the immutable linkage between consecutive blocks. However, it is not a pure hash chain in the Lamport sense. Each block B_n in the chain contains, among other data (like transactions), the hash digest d_{n-1} of the *preceding* block B_{n-1}. The hash digest for block B_n, denoted d_n, is then computed by applying the hash function H to the contents of B_n, which critically includes d_{n-1}. This can be represented as $d_n = H(\text{Header}_n)$, where Header_n incorporates d_{n-1} along with other block-specific information (e.g., timestamp, nonce, Merkle root). If concatenation (||) is used to combine block data b_n and the previous hash d_{n-1}, the relationship may be simplified as $d_n \approx H(b_n || d_{n-1})$, as depicted in Fig. 1.2. Altering any data within a prior block B_k would change its hash d_k, thereby invalidating the hash pointer stored in the subsequent block B_{k+1} and breaking the chain integrity requiring the computationally prohibitive task of recalculating all subsequent blocks.

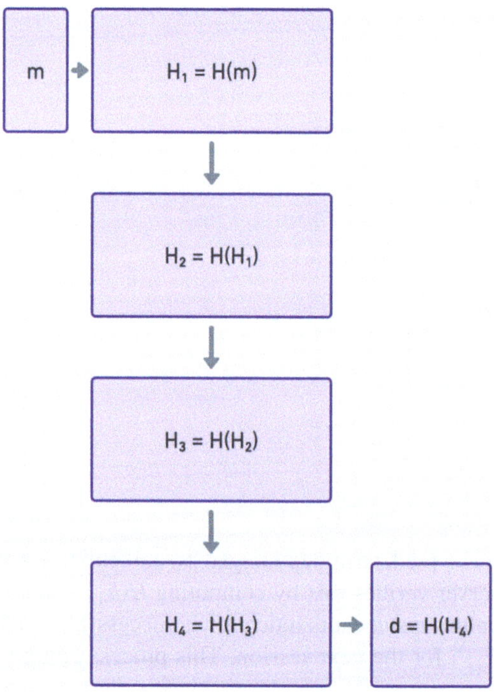

Fig. 1.2 Illustration of hash-based block linking in a blockchain. Each block's hash *dn* depends on its own contents *bn* and the hash *dn* − 1 of the preceding block

1.1.3 Merkle Trees

A *Merkle tree* or hash tree is a hierarchical data structure used to efficiently summarize and verify the integrity of large datasets. It extends the concept of hash chains to tree structures, typically binary trees. In a standard Merkle tree, the leaf nodes contain the cryptographic hash digests of individual data chunks (e.g., transactions tx_i, so $L_i = H(tx_i)$). Each internal node N stores the hash digest computed from the concatenation of the digests of its child nodes. For a binary tree node N with children N_{left} and N_{right}, its value is $N = H(N_{\text{left}} || N_{\text{right}})$. This process continues recursively up the tree, culminating in a single hash value at the top, the *Merkle root*, which serves as a compact representation of the entire dataset. Figure 1.3 shows an example. If the number of nodes at a level is odd, the last node is typically duplicated and hashed with itself to maintain the binary structure.

Merkle trees enable highly efficient proof of membership (or inclusion proofs). To demonstrate that a specific data block tx_k is part of the dataset represented by a known Merkle root R, one only needs to provide the hash $L_k = H(tx_k)$ and the sequence of sibling hashes along the path from L_k to the root R. This collection of required sibling hashes is known as the *Merkle proof* or audit path. A verifier can use L_k and the provided sibling hashes to recompute the hashes iteratively up the path. If the final computed root matches the known, trusted root R, the membership of tx_k is confirmed. For a tree with N leaves, the size of the proof and the verification complexity are logarithmic, i.e. $O(\log N)$. This mechanism is integral to Bitcoin. The Merkle root of all transactions included in a block is stored in the block header. This allows lightweight clients operating under the Simplified Payment Verification

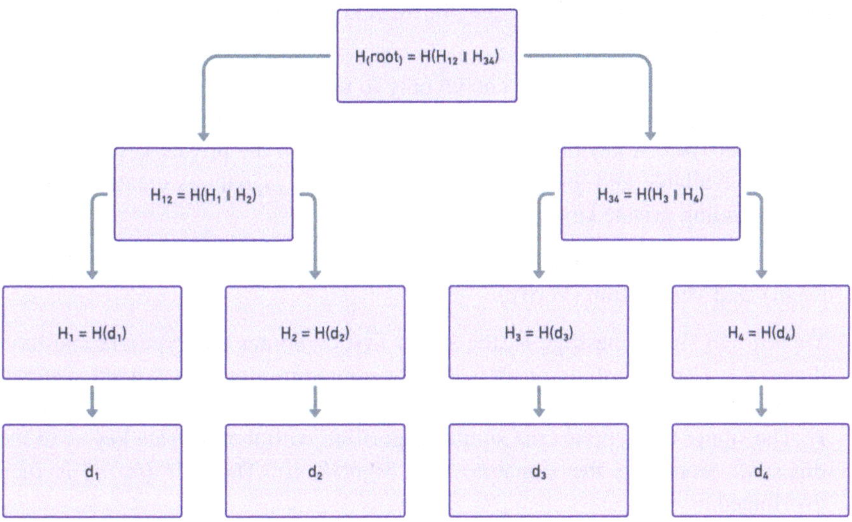

Fig. 1.3 Example of a binary Merkle Tree constructed over four data blocks (leaves d_1 to d_4). Internal nodes contain hashes of concatenated child hashes, culminating in the Merkle Root

(SPV) model, to verify the inclusion of a specific transaction without downloading the entire block content. They only require the block headers (which contain the Merkle roots) and the specific Merkle proof for the transaction of interest, obtained from a full node. Ethereum utilizes a more sophisticated variant called the *Merkle Patricia Trie (MPT)*. An MPT combines properties of Merkle trees (hashing for integrity) and Patricia tries (prefix trees or radix trees, enabling efficient lookups, insertions, and deletions). Ethereum employs MPTs to manage three distinct state components within each block:

- *State Trie*: Encodes the global state of all accounts (balances, nonces, code, storage) at the conclusion of the block's execution. Its root hash represents the overall state.
- *Transaction Trie*: Stores the transactions included within the block. Its root hash confirms the set of transactions processed.
- *Receipts Trie*: Contains transaction receipts, which include outcomes and logs generated during transaction execution (e.g., gas used, events emitted). Its root hash verifies the results of transaction processing.

The use of MPTs offers advantages such as efficient state updates, deterministic root hashes independent of transaction order, and efficient state proofs.

1.1.4 Digital Signatures

A *digital signature* scheme provides the cryptographic analog to a handwritten signature, offering authenticity, data integrity, and non-repudiation for digital messages. It relies on asymmetric (public-key) cryptography, utilizing a pair of mathematically related keys:

- *Private Key (sk):* A secret key known only to the signer, used to generate signatures. It is typically generated randomly from a large space.
- *Public Key (pk):* A key derived algorithmically from the private key. It is made publicly available and used by verifiers to validate signatures created with the corresponding private key.

- The process typically involves three algorithms: Key Generation (Gen), Signing (Sign), and Verification (Verify).

1. *Signing*: To sign a message m, the signer first computes its cryptographic hash digest $d = H(m)$. Hashing ensures that the signature input has a fixed size and binds the signature to the specific message content via the collision resistance of H. The signer then applies the signing algorithm with their private key sk to the digest d, producing the signature $\sigma = \text{Sign}(sk, d)$. The pair (m, σ) is then distributed.
2. *Verification*: A verifier, possessing the signer's public key pk, the message m, and the signature σ, performs the verification. They first recompute the digest

$d' = H(m)$ from the received message. Then, they use the verification algorithm with the public key pk, the computed digest d', and the signature σ. The algorithm Verify(pk, d', σ) outputs either "accept" or "reject." Acceptance confirms that σ is a valid signature on m generated by the owner of sk corresponding to pk.

The security goal is typically existential unforgeability under chosen-message attacks (EUF-CMA), meaning an adversary cannot forge a valid signature for any new message, even after obtaining signatures for other messages of their choice.

Numerous public-key signature algorithms exist. Within the blockchain sphere, the *Elliptic Curve Digital Signature Algorithm (ECDSA)* (Johnson et al., 2001) is prevalent. ECDSA's security is predicated on the presumed computational difficulty of the Elliptic Curve Discrete Logarithm Problem (ECDLP) over specific finite fields. Solving $P = k \cdot G$ for the integer k, given points P and G (a base point or generator) on a chosen elliptic curve, is believed to be computationally hard.

Both Bitcoin and Ethereum utilize ECDSA, specifically employing the elliptic curve known as *secp256k1*. User addresses in these systems are derived from the ECDSA public key, though through slightly different procedures. Typically, the public key pk is hashed (often multiple times, sometimes combined with version bytes and checksums, e.g. Base58Check encoding in Bitcoin) to generate the public address used for receiving funds. This hashing adds a layer of indirection, potentially enhancing privacy (the public key itself is not revealed until a transaction is sent from the address) and yielding shorter, more manageable addresses.

1.2 The Blockchain Paradigm

The concept of the blockchain gained prominence with the publication of the Bitcoin whitepaper by the pseudonymous Satoshi Nakamoto in 2008 (Nakamoto, 2008). It integrates peer-to-peer (P2P) networking with the cryptographic primitives discussed earlier (hash functions, digital signatures, and Merkle trees) to realize a distributed, tamper-evident digital ledger without reliance on a central coordinating authority. While "blockchain" denotes a general technological pattern, Bitcoin and Ethereum stand as the most significant and influential implementations to date.

In virtually all blockchain systems, the ledger is structured as a chronologically ordered sequence of blocks, cryptographically linked using hash pointers as previously described (Fig. 1.2). Data, typically in the form of transactions, is appended to this ledger by network participants. To have a transaction included in a block and thus permanently recorded, users broadcast it to the P2P network. Inclusion usually requires associating a transaction fee, payable in the network's native *cryptocurrency* (e.g., Bitcoin (BTC) in the Bitcoin network, Ether (ETH) in Ethereum). This cryptocurrency serves both as an incentive mechanism and as the unit of account tracked by the distributed ledger itself. The integrity, consistency, and validity of the blockchain's state are maintained through a *consensus mechanism*. This mechanism defines the rules by which the distributed network participants agree on which blocks are valid and should be appended to the canonical chain. Effective consensus ensures that despite the distributed nature and potential presence of malicious actors, all honest participants eventually converge on a single, consistent version of the ledger history. Numerous consensus protocols exist (e.g., Proof-of-Work (PoW), Proof-of-Stake (PoS)), each with different trade-offs regarding security, performance, and energy consumption. A common characteristic, particularly in permissionless systems like Bitcoin (using PoW), is that reaching consensus can be computationally intensive or resource-demanding. This deliberate inefficiency often serves as a Sybil resistance mechanism and makes rewriting history prohibitively expensive. For example, under PoW, numerous nodes (miners) expend significant computational effort competing to solve a cryptographic puzzle, and the network collectively validates the solution. This redundancy, while costly, underpins the security model. This computationally demanding operational model gained traction primarily because it offers a solution to the long-standing *double-spending problem* in digital cash systems without resorting to a trusted third party. By making the ledger publicly verifiable and extremely difficult to alter retrospectively, blockchain technology enables secure peer-to-peer transfer of digital value.

1.3 Addressing the Double-Spending Vulnerability in Digital Systems

The phenomenon known as *double-spending* represents a critical security challenge inherent in digital value transfer systems. It pertains to the potential for a malicious entity to expend the same unit of digital currency or asset multiple times. This vulnerability stems directly from the nature of digital information, which, unlike physical tokens, can be replicated with perfect fidelity at negligible cost. The ease with which digital data can be duplicated undermines the fundamental principle of scarcity required for a functioning monetary system.

Historically, the predominant mitigation strategy involved the intermediation of a trusted third party (TTP), typically a financial institution or a centralized server operator. This central authority maintains an authoritative ledger recording all account balances and transaction histories. Every transaction must be routed through and validated by this TTP, which verifies the availability of funds and updates the ledger accordingly. While effective in preventing double-spending under normal operation, this centralized architecture introduces significant systemic risks. It constitutes a single point of failure; the TTP's continuous availability, operational integrity, and resistance to compromise are paramount. Furthermore, it necessitates users placing absolute trust in the TTP's honesty and competence in securing sensitive financial data.

Several cryptographic protocols have been proposed to alleviate the complete dependence on a central intermediary. A noteworthy early contribution is David Chaum's ECash protocol, introduced in 1982, which utilized RSA-based blind signatures (Chaum, 1982). While ECash did not eliminate the central authority (the "bank"), it aimed to enhance user privacy and reduce the bank's observational power during transactions. In this system, the bank issues digital coins by applying a blind signature to user-provided data. The blinding process ensures the bank signs the coin's value representation without learning its unique identifier, thus rendering the issued coin anonymous and untraceable back to the originating user by the bank itself. Users could theoretically exchange these signed coins directly, even offline. However, for settlement, the recipient needed to present the coin to the bank for verification and deposit. Double-spending was fully prevented only when the bank was online to check its database of spent coins. Offline detection was limited; if the same coin was presented multiple times to the same recipient, the duplication would be evident, but spending the same coin with different offline recipients remained a vulnerability until reconciliation with the bank. Blockchain technology fundamentally reconceptualizes the solution by eliminating the need for a single TTP. Instead, it relies on a distributed network of participants who collectively maintain and validate a shared, replicated ledger. Transaction validity, including the prevention of double-spending, is achieved through consensus protocols. When a user attempts to broadcast a transaction spending funds already utilized in a prior confirmed transaction, the network participants, following the protocol rules, will identify the attempt as invalid based on the shared ledger history. Such invalid transactions are rejected and never incorporated into the canonical blockchain record.

Despite the robustness of the consensus mechanism, transient inconsistencies, known as *forks*, can temporarily occur in blockchain networks, potentially leading to ephemeral double-spending scenarios. A fork arises when two or more valid blocks are proposed by different network participants at approximately the same height (i.e., extending the same preceding block) nearly simultaneously. This results in a temporary divergence of the chain into multiple competing branches, each considered valid by a subset of the network. Most blockchain protocols, particularly those employing Proof-of-Work (PoW) like Bitcoin, resolve forks probabilistically by adhering to the "longest chain rule" (or a variant like heaviest chain). Participants build upon the chain branch that grows the fastest, eventually orphaning the shorter branch(es). Consequently, a transaction included in a block on a branch that is later orphaned is effectively reversed. To mitigate the risk of relying on a transaction that might be reversed due to a fork, recipients typically wait for a certain number of subsequent blocks, known as *confirmations*, to be added atop the block containing their transaction. This waiting period increases the statistical probability that the transaction is part of the canonical, enduring chain. In Bitcoin, a common heuristic suggests waiting for 6 confirmations (approximately 60 min) for reasonable assurance of finality. Ethereum, following its transition to Proof-of-Stake (PoS), incorporates mechanisms that provide faster cryptographic finality, typically achieved within approximately 15 min, after which a block is considered irreversible barring catastrophic network failures.

1.4 Fundamental Characteristics of Blockchain Systems

The term "blockchain" is frequently associated with a set of defining attributes. The most salient of these are elaborated below:

- *Decentralized*: Blockchain networks operate without a central governing body or intermediary exercising control. Network rules are codified within the protocol software, and governance mechanisms, where they exist, are often distributed among participants. No single entity possesses unilateral power to alter the protocol or censor valid transactions arbitrarily. All nodes adhering to the protocol interact as peers.
- *Distributed*: The system's computational workload (e.g., transaction validation, block production) and data storage (the ledger) are replicated across numerous geographically dispersed nodes connected via a peer-to-peer (P2P) network. This redundancy enhances fault tolerance and resilience; the failure of individual nodes does not compromise the overall operation of the network.
- *Immutable*: Once transaction data is validated, bundled into a block, and added to the chain according to the consensus rules, it becomes computationally infeasible to alter or delete it without detection. This property is primarily achieved through cryptographic hashing, where each block contains a hash of the preceding block, creating a verifiable chain. Modifying historical data would require recomputing subsequent blocks and achieving consensus acceptance, an operation generally considered prohibitively expensive (51% attack). Note that finality mechanisms (e.g., in PoS) provide stronger guarantees of immutability than the probabilistic finality of PoW.
- *Permissionless*: In permissionless (or public) blockchains (e.g., Bitcoin, Ethereum), any individual or entity can join the network, participate in its operations (e.g., validating transactions, proposing blocks, running a node), and utilize its services without requiring prior authorization from any authority.
- *Permissioned*: Conversely, permissioned (or private/consortium) blockchains restrict participation. Actors must obtain explicit authorization or credentials to access the network and perform specific roles. These systems are often employed in enterprise or B2B contexts where regulatory compliance, privacy, and controlled access are paramount. Hyperledger Fabric[1] serves as a prominent example, alongside others like R3 Corda.
- *Transparent*: In most public blockchains, the ledger data, including transaction details (sender address, receiver address, amount, timestamp) and block information, is publicly accessible. Anyone with an Internet connection can typically download the blockchain data using client software or inspect it through web-based block explorers. However, transparency pertains to the transaction data itself, not necessarily the real-world identities behind the addresses.

[1] Hyperledger Fabric is a modular framework designed for enterprise blockchain solutions: https://www.hyperledger.org/projects/fabric

- *Pseudoanonymous*: Users interact with the blockchain through cryptographic addresses (derived from public keys), not through verified real-world identities. While transactions are transparently linked to these addresses, the connection between an address and a specific individual or entity is not inherently part of the protocol. This provides a degree of privacy, termed pseudonymity. However, external analysis or linking on-chain activity with off-chain data can potentially deanonymize participants.
- *Account-based*: Certain blockchains, like Ethereum, employ an account-based model. The system's state is represented by accounts, each associated with an address, a balance (of the native cryptocurrency and potentially other tokens), storage, and code (for smart contracts). Transactions trigger state transitions, directly debiting the sender's account and crediting the receiver's account. Authorization to initiate transactions from an account requires control over the corresponding private key.
- *UTXO-based*: Other blockchains, notably Bitcoin, utilize the Unspent Transaction Output (UTXO) model. There are no explicit accounts with balances in the ledger state. Instead, the system tracks individual units of value locked in transaction outputs that have not yet been spent. A transaction consumes one or more existing UTXOs (by providing cryptographic proof of ownership via private keys) and creates one or more new UTXOs. A user's balance is implicitly the sum of the values of all UTXOs they control (i.e., for which they hold the private key needed to unlock them). This model can offer enhanced privacy potential, as users can generate new addresses for receiving each UTXO.

1.5 Fundamental Principles and Architectural Framework of Blockchain Systems

Blockchain technology represents a paradigm shift in distributed data management, predicated on cryptographic principles and decentralized network architectures. This section elucidates the core components and architectural underpinnings that enable its unique properties of immutability, transparency, and resilience.

1.5.1 Core Components of Blockchain Technology

The operational efficacy of a blockchain relies upon several foundational constructs:

- *Blocks*: These are the fundamental data structures within a blockchain, serving as containers for batches of validated transactions. Each block is cryptographically linked to its immediate predecessor via a hash pointer, forming a sequential, tamper-evident chain. A block typically comprises a header, containing metadata such as the hash of the previous block, a timestamp, a nonce (a value used in the

consensus process, particularly Proof-of-Work), and a Merkle root summarizing the transactions contained within, alongside the block body which lists the actual transactions (IBM, n.d.; Kaushal et al., 2021). The cryptographic hashing ensures the integrity of the block's content and its linkage within the chain.
- *Transactions*: Within the blockchain context, transactions signify any operation that modifies the state of the ledger. While commonly associated with value transfers (e.g., cryptocurrencies), they can represent diverse interactions, including the execution of smart contract functions, asset registration, or the recording of arbitrary data. Structurally, a transaction typically includes sender and receiver identifiers (addresses), the value or data being transferred, cryptographic signatures for authentication, and potentially associated script logic (Gupta et al., 2021; Sinha & Bathla, 2019). Transactions are broadcast to the network for validation and subsequent inclusion in a block.
- *Decentralization*: A defining characteristic of blockchain is the distribution of control and data maintenance across a network of independent nodes, eliminating reliance on a central intermediary or authority. Each participating node (or a subset thereof, e.g. full nodes) typically maintains a complete or partial replica of the entire ledger. This distributed architecture enhances system resilience against single points of failure, promotes transparency as the ledger is shared, and increases resistance to censorship or unilateral control (Gupta et al., 2021; Kaushal et al., 2021).
- *Consensus Mechanisms*: These are protocols that enable distributed nodes in the network to reach agreement on the validity of transactions and the canonical state of the shared ledger, even in the presence of potentially faulty or malicious actors. Proof-of-Work (PoW), a widely recognized mechanism, requires participants (miners) to expend computational resources solving complex cryptographic puzzles. The first miner to find a valid solution gets to propose the next block. Other mechanisms, such as Proof-of-Stake (PoS) or Proof-of-Authority (PoA), utilize different criteria (e.g., stake ownership, verified identity) to determine block proposers. These algorithms are crucial for maintaining the consistency and security of the blockchain against attacks like double-spending (Gupta et al., 2021; Kaushal et al., 2021).

1.5.2 Architectural Pillars of Blockchain Systems

The system architecture is meticulously designed to instantiate and support the core principles of decentralization, data integrity (immutability), and operational transparency.

- *Distributed Ledger Technology (DLT)*: This foundational technology facilitates a replicated, shared, and synchronized digital ledger across the network. Every authorized participant gains access to a consistent view of the recorded transactions, eliminating data silos and discrepancies inherent in traditional centralized database systems. Data propagation and synchronization protocols ensure that updates are consistently applied across participating nodes (IBM, n.d.; Gupta et al., 2021).

- *Immutable Records*: Immutability refers to the property that once transactional data is validated and appended to the blockchain via consensus, it becomes computationally infeasible to alter or delete it retrospectively. This is achieved through the cryptographic hashing that links blocks sequentially; modifying a historical block would invalidate its hash and necessitate recalculating all subsequent blocks, an endeavor that is practically impossible given the required computational power and the need to regain network consensus (IBM, n.d.). Any corrections or reversals must be recorded as new, subsequent transactions.
- *Smart Contracts*: These are self-executing scripts or programs deployed directly onto the blockchain. The terms of an agreement or operational logic are encoded within the contract's code. Execution is triggered by specific conditions or transactions and is automatically enforced by the blockchain network according to the predefined rules. This eliminates ambiguity and the need for traditional intermediaries, thereby increasing efficiency, reducing counterparty risk, and enabling complex decentralized applications (dApps) and Decentralized Autonomous Organizations (DAOs) (IBM, n.d.; Sinha & Bathla, 2019).
- *Security Measures*: Cryptography is integral to blockchain security. Asymmetric (public-key) cryptography is employed for identity management (via public/private key pairs) and transaction authorization (via digital signatures), ensuring authenticity and non-repudiation. Cryptographic hash functions (e.g., SHA-256) are vital for ensuring data integrity within blocks (via Merkle trees) and for creating the immutable chain linkage between blocks. These techniques collectively safeguard transactions against unauthorized access, tampering, and fraudulent activities (Kaushal et al., 2021; Sinha & Bathla, 2019).
- *Peer-to-Peer (P2P) Network*: Blockchains operate on a distributed network topology where nodes communicate directly with each other without relying on central servers. This P2P architecture facilitates the broadcasting of new transactions and blocks across the network (often using gossip protocols), enabling collaborative validation and consensus attainment. The direct interaction fosters trust and enhances system resilience, as the network can continue operating even if some nodes go offline (Gupta et al., 2021; Sinha & Bathla, 2019).

1.5.3 Operational Workflow of Blockchain Transactions

The functioning of a blockchain involves a sequence of steps designed to ensure secure, transparent, and verifiable transaction processing. This subsection details this operational sequence.

Transaction Lifecycle and Block Formation

1. *Transaction Initiation*: A user initiates a transaction using client software (e.g., a wallet). This process involves creating a transaction message specifying details like the recipient's address, the amount or data being transferred, and any associated fees. Crucially, the transaction is digitally signed using the initiator's private key. This signature serves as cryptographic proof of ownership and authorization, verifiable by anyone using the corresponding public key (Kaushal et al., 2021).
2. *Transaction Broadcasting and Aggregation*: The signed transaction is broadcast to the P2P network. Nodes receive and independently validate the transaction based on predefined protocol rules (e.g., checking signature validity, verifying sufficient funds). Valid transactions are typically added to a temporary holding area known as the memory pool (mempool) (IBM, n.d.).
3. *Block Construction and Hashing*: Network participants tasked with block creation (e.g., miners in PoW, validators in PoS) select transactions from the mempool, often prioritizing based on associated fees or other criteria, and assemble them into a new candidate block. A cryptographic hash of the block's contents (including a Merkle root summarizing all transactions) is computed. Furthermore, the hash of the most recent block on the current canonical chain is included in the new block's header, establishing the sequential link (IBM, n.d.; Sinha & Bathla, 2019), a schematic representation of block creation is shown in Fig. 1.4 Secure hash algorithms like SHA-256 are commonly employed for their collision resistance and deterministic output, ensuring data integrity and enabling efficient verification.

Achieving Network-Wide Agreement: The Consensus Process

4. *Transaction Validation by Network Nodes*: As transactions propagate through the network, each receiving node performs its own validation checks. This distributed verification ensures that only transactions conforming to the protocol rules

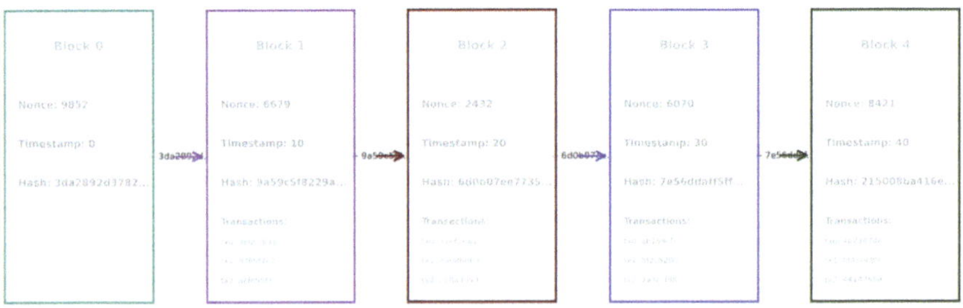

Fig. 1.4 Conceptual illustration of blockchain structure: depicting the chronological linkage of blocks via cryptographic hashes

are considered for inclusion in the blockchain (GeeksforGeeks, n.d.; Sinha & Bathla, 2019).

5. *Block Proposal via Consensus Mechanism*: To add a new block to the chain, network consensus must be achieved. In PoW systems, miners compete to solve a computationally intensive cryptographic puzzle (e.g., finding a nonce value such that the hash of the block header meets a specific difficulty target). This process consumes significant computational power and time, acting as a Sybil resistance mechanism (GeeksforGeeks, n.d.; Kaushal et al., 2021). The first miner to find a valid solution broadcasts the proposed block (including the solution) to the network.
6. *Block Validation and Chain Extension*: Upon receiving a proposed block, other nodes verify its validity: they check the solution to the puzzle (if applicable), validate all included transactions, and confirm that the block correctly references the previous block's hash. If the block is deemed valid according to the consensus rules, nodes accept it and append it to their local copy of the blockchain, extending the chain (GeeksforGeeks, n.d.). The successful block proposer is typically rewarded with newly created cryptocurrency units and transaction fees from the included transactions.
7. *Ensuring Blockchain Integrity*: The sequential cryptographic linking of blocks, where each block contains the hash of its predecessor, forms the core of the blockchain's immutability. Any attempt to tamper with data in a historical block would alter its hash, consequently invalidating the hash pointer stored in the subsequent block, and this invalidation would cascade through all following blocks. Reconciling such a change would require re-computing the PoW (or equivalent consensus validation) for the altered block and all subsequent blocks at a rate faster than the rest of the network, an endeavor generally considered computationally infeasible, thus preserving the integrity and chronological consistency of the ledger (Kaushal et al., 2021; Sinha & Bathla, 2019).

1.6 Applications of Blockchain

Blockchain technology has evolved significantly since its initial development as the foundational framework for Bitcoin. Presently, it has been adopted across a diverse array of sectors including finance, healthcare, logistics, energy, and beyond. The core attributes of blockchain, decentralization, transparency, and immutability, render it a transformative solution for industries seeking to enhance operational efficiency and streamline processes. Within the financial sector, blockchain is being leveraged for applications such as digital identity verification, cross-border payment systems, and the facilitation of faster, more secure transaction settlements. Similarly, the healthcare industry stands to benefit from blockchain's tamper-resistant recordkeeping capabilities, which enable secure and efficient sharing of medical data among healthcare providers. In logistics, blockchain offers a robust mechanism for supply chain management by maintaining a transparent and secure ledger of goods as they progress through various stages of the supply chain. The energy sector is also exploring blockchain's potential to foster a more efficient and decentralized energy ecosystem. Also, blockchain can enable peer-to-peer energy trading allowing energy producers to directly sell surplus energy to consumers, thereby eliminating the need for intermediaries. These examples in Fig. 1.5 represent only a fraction of blockchain's extensive applications. By enhancing transparency, mitigating fraud, and reducing operational costs, blockchain is poised to continue driving disruption across industries and creating new avenues for innovation.

The transformative potential of blockchain technology is particularly evident within the financial services sector. Blockchain-based platforms offer the prospect of disrupting conventional banking paradigms through the provision of expedited, cost-effective, and fortified transaction processes. Furthermore, they facilitate the development of novel financial services, encompassing peer-to-peer lending, microfinance initiatives, and remittance systems. Beyond finance, supply chain management stands as another domain ripe for blockchain integration. The implementation of blockchain-enabled platforms enables the comprehensive tracking of goods, from provenance to destination, thereby enhancing transparency and mitigating the incidence of fraudulent activities. This contributes to heightened operational efficiency, reduced logistical costs, and bolstered inter-party trust. Moreover, blockchain technology exhibits utility in the augmentation of voting systems, fostering heightened transparency, security, and verifiability. Blockchain-based platforms can preclude electoral tampering, ensure voter anonymity, and enable secure storage and retrieval of electoral data. In addition to these applications, blockchain technology holds promise across diverse sectors, including identity management, healthcare, real estate, gaming, and energy management. Consequently, the spectrum of potential blockchain applications is extensive, and the emergence of further innovative use cases is anticipated.

1.6.1 Blockchain in Healthcare

Blockchain technology offers a potential solution for the secure and private storage of sensitive patient data within the healthcare sector, encompassing medical records, imaging, and related documentation. These data necessitate robust security and privacy

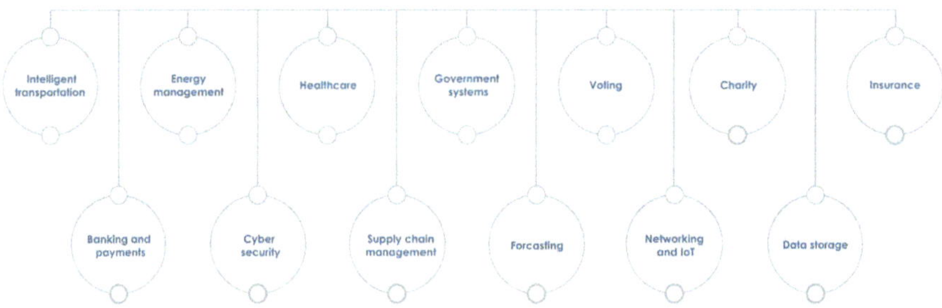

Fig. 1.5 Blockchain applications

protocols while maintaining accessibility for authorized personnel. An implementation of blockchain can effectively address these requirements. While a Bitcoin-based healthcare model can facilitate individual health data storage, limitations exist regarding bandwidth efficiency and distributed network resource management. A more efficacious approach involves the integration of an access control manager coupled with a database management system for instance storage. This architecture enables authorized administrators to retrieve encrypted and time-stamped records via unique identifiers that map to their storage locations. The aggregate of blockchain-stored data, often referred to as a data lake, constitutes a critical resource for data-driven healthcare initiatives. The application of blockchain technology in the management of Electronic Medical Records (EMRs), also known as Electronic Health Records (EHRs) or Personal Health Records (PHRs), has garnered substantial research interest. These records, which encompass electronically generated, stored, and managed patient medical data, represent a primary focus of blockchain-based healthcare solutions. A significant proportion of the extant literature, specifically 32 out of 65 selected studies, explores the utilization of blockchain for EMR management. A brief scoping of healthcare aspects in blockchain are shown in Fig. 1.6 The inherent characteristics of blockchain, including decentralization, immutability, data provenance, reliability, robustness, smart contract functionality, security, and privacy, are frequently cited as justifications for its suitability in this context. Furthermore, research efforts are directed toward enabling patient-centric data sharing among diverse healthcare stakeholders, such as providers, researchers, and insurers. In accordance with regulatory frameworks such as the European General Data Protection Regulation (GDPR), which mandates explicit patient consent for sensitive personal data processing, blockchain is proposed as a

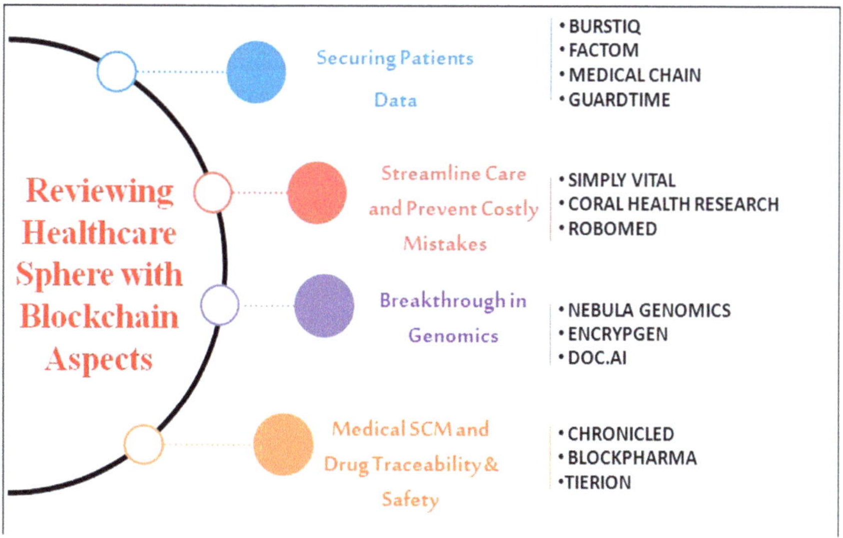

Fig. 1.6 Healthcare applications using Blockchain based on (Jeelani et al., 2024)

mechanism to empower patients with control over the sharing, processing, and utilization of their data within healthcare platforms.

The application of blockchain technology in electronic medical records management has garnered significant attention, with several initiatives demonstrating its potential. Guardtime, for instance, employs a blockchain-based platform to secure over one million patient records in Estonia, frequently cited as a paradigmatic example of blockchain implementation in this domain (Angraal et al., 2017; Mettler, 2016). Similarly, the MedRec project, a collaborative effort between the MIT Media Lab and Beth Israel Deaconess Medical Center, seeks to enhance patient autonomy by enabling granular access control over personal health data via a blockchain infrastructure (Azaria et al., 2016). Furthermore, the Global Health Network (GHN), developed by Gem on the Ethereum platform, facilitates shared data access among healthcare professionals (Azaria et al., 2016). Healthbank, a Swiss digital health company, also leverages blockchain to empower patients with comprehensive data control (Azaria et al., 2016). Engelhardt (2017) highlights the Medicalchain project, which aims to enable secure international medical record sharing, and the Healthcoin initiative, focused on developing a global EMRs system. Beyond these, numerous entities, including Factom, HealthCombix, Patientory, SimplyVital, IBM's Watson, BurstIQ, Bowhead, QBRICS, and Nuco, are actively pursuing blockchain-based solutions for patient-centric EMRs systems (Engelhardt, 2017).

1.6.2 Blockchain in Climate Change

Global climate change characterized by escalating temperatures presents an exigent challenge of increasing international concern. Anthropogenic greenhouse gas emissions are the principal driver of this phenomenon, with projections indicating a potential 2.8 °C temperature rise by 2050 in the absence of substantial mitigation efforts within the current decade. Blockchain technology has been proposed as a mechanism for mitigating this crisis by constraining human activities that exacerbate greenhouse gas concentrations. Deforestation driven by industrial and agricultural practices diminishes atmospheric carbon dioxide sequestration, thereby contributing to its accumulation. Blockchain-based solutions, by optimizing digital processes and reducing reliance on paper-based systems may curtail these activities. Furthermore, the implementation of blockchain technologies by 2030 is posited to potentially achieve a reduction in global warming of at least 4 °C by 2050. Analyses of the Reducing Emissions from Deforestation and Forest Degradation (REDD+) project have identified limitations that can be addressed through blockchain applications, including cryptocarbon management, green finance, and sustainable investment frameworks. A spectrum of climate-focused blockchain initiatives is currently under development. For instance, SolarCoin utilizes a blockchain platform to incentivize solar energy generation by distributing tokens proportional to megawatt-hour production, which can be utilized as a medium of exchange. Similarly, platforms such as Earth Dollar are designed to integrate carbon credits with blockchain tokens, facilitating the trade of emissions permits. The application of automated smart contract protocols enables the quantification of embodied carbon emissions associated with consumer transactions and the subsequent automated procurement of carbon offsets. Veridium Labs, a Hong Kong-based private entity in collaboration with IBM exemplifies this approach by linking its payment system, VerdePay, to carbon credits generated from Infinite Earth's Rimba Raya forest reserve in Central Kalimantan.

References

Angraal, S., Krumholz, H., & Schulz, W. (2017). Blockchain technology applications in health care. *Circulation: Cardiovascular Quality and Outcomes, 10*, e003800.

Azaria, A., Ekblaw, A., Vieira, T. & Lippman, A. (2016). *Medrec: Using blockchain for medical data access and permission management*, 25–30 (Vienna, Austria).

Buterin, V. (2013). *Ethereum white paper: A next generation smart contract & decentralized application platform*. Tech. Rep. URL https://github.com/ethereum/wiki/wiki/White-Paper

Chaum, D. (1982). *Blind signatures for untraceable payments* (pp. 199–203). Springer.

Engelhardt, M. (2017). Hitching healthcare to the chain: An introduction to blockchain technology in the healthcare sector. *Technological Innovation Management Review, 7*, 22–34.

GeeksforGeeks. (n.d.) *How does the blockchain work?* https://www.geeksforgeeks.org/how-does-the-blockchain-work/

Gupta, V. C., Gabadia, S., Agarwal, M., & Samdani, K. (2021). *An intrinsic review on securitization using blockchain* (pp. 971–976). IEEE.

IBM. (n.d.) *Blockchain technology*. https://www.ibm.com/topics/blockchain

Jeelani, O. F., Njie, M., & Korzhuk, M. V. (2024). *Enhancing data privacy and data security across healthcare*.

Johnson, D., Menezes, A., & Vanstone, S. (2001). The elliptic curve digital signature algorithm (ecdsa). *International Journal of Information Security, 1*, 36–63.

Kaushal, R. K., Kumar, N., Panda, S. N., & Kukreja, V. (2021). *Immutable smart contracts on blockchain technology: Its benefits and barriers* (pp. 1–5). IEEE.

Lamport, L. (1981). Password authentication with insecure communication. *Communications of the ACM, 24*, 770–772.

Mettler, M. (2016). *Blockchain technology in healthcare: The revolution starts here* (Munich, Germany), pp. 520–522.

Nakamoto, S. (2008). *Bitcoin: A peer-to-peer electronic cash system*. Tech. Rep. https://bitcoin.org/bitcoin.pdf

Rogaway, P., & Shrimpton, T. (1979). *Cryptographic hash-function basics: Definitions, implications, and separations for preimage resistance, second-preimage resistance, and collision resistance* (Vol. 3017, pp. 371–388). Springer.

Sinha, S. K., & Bathla, R. (2019). *Implementation of blockchain in financial sector to improve scalability* (pp. 144–148). IEEE.

Amit Kumar Jaiswal A computer scientist and AI researcher specializes in quantum-inspired information retrieval, machine learning, and multimodal search. A recipient of Marie Skłodowska-Curie Fellow, he earned his Ph.D. from the University of Bedfordshire and has conducted AI-driven research at University College London, University of Surrey, and a visiting researcher at the University of Cambridge in AI for healthcare. He also worked at the University of Leeds with industry partners Credit Suisse and Finastra, developing synthetic data models for financial markets. He is currently a faculty chair of Jay Chaudhry Software innovation centre at IIT (BHU) Varanasi.

Chapter 2
The Background of Blockchain Analytics

Tao Tang

2.1 Introduction

Blockchain analytics is rapidly becoming a defining element of the modern data-driven economy, enabling a deeper understanding of activities that occur on decentralized networks. Unlike traditional data analysis, where data is typically consolidated in centralized databases maintained by individual companies or institutions, blockchain analytics must grapple with the unique properties of a distributed ledger (Mafrur, 2025). In such an environment, each transaction is recorded across a network of nodes, making it both transparent and immutable. This foundational characteristic reshapes the way data can be collected, processed, interpreted, and leveraged for strategic insights. Consequently, blockchain analytics has emerged as a specialized discipline, integrating techniques from computer science, statistics, economics, and cryptography (Bartoletti et al., 2017; Xu et al., 2018).

At the core of blockchain analytics lies the recognition that every on-chain action, whether a simple wallet-to-wallet payment, an invocation of a smart contract, or the minting of a new digital asset, leaves a permanent, cryptographically signed record (Alqassem et al., 2020; McGinn et al., 2018; Sharma et al., 2022). Analysts and stakeholders, ranging from researchers to regulators, can trace these records across time, providing an unprecedented level of data verifiability. This transparency creates opportunities for novel risk assessments, compliance checks, and forensic investigations (Kaplanov, 2012). Simultaneously, however, blockchain networks are heterogeneous: different protocols (e.g., Bitcoin, Ethereum, Polkadot) exhibit distinct transaction models, consensus mechanisms, and data structures. As a result, blockchain analytics requires specialized tools and domain expertise to

T. Tang (✉)
Surrey Academy for Blockchain and Metaverse Applications, Surrey Business School, University of Surrey, Guildford, UK
e-mail: t.tang@surrey.ac.uk

Y. Xiong (ed.), *Blockchain Analytics for Practitioners*, Business Analytics in Practice, https://doi.org/10.1007/978-3-032-06046-4_2

accurately parse, clean, and interpret data from a spectrum of sources (Feltovic, 2024; Kuzuno & Karam, 2017).

The importance of blockchain analytics has grown commensurately with the increased adoption of decentralized finance (DeFi), non-fungible tokens (NFTs), and enterprise-level blockchain solutions for supply chain and logistics (Carapella et al., 2022; Schueffel, 2021). On one hand, analytics serves as a window into user behaviors, network health, and protocol performance. On the other, it fosters greater accountability in a space that champions anonymity yet must address compliance and fraud detection. The tasks of identifying suspicious flows of funds, verifying asset provenance, and estimating market liquidity now hinge on advanced analytical frameworks (Cui et al., 2024; Hellani et al., 2021). Meanwhile, academic researchers see in blockchain data a treasure trove for studying decentralized governance, cryptoeconomic incentives, and digital asset price formation. By combining on-chain data with off-chain information, such as exchange rates, or real-world events, analysts can derive comprehensive insights that power business decisions, inform regulations, and shape the academic discourse around emerging forms of economic organization (Cai et al., 2023; Hepp et al., 2018).

In the following subsections, the fundamental nature of blockchain analytics will be explored, highlighting the differences from traditional data analysis and the implications of decentralized data structures. Then the various use cases of blockchain analytics across finance, supply chain, and cutting-edge areas like DeFi and NFTs will be discussed (Ante, 2022, 2023; Gunay & Kaskaloglu, 2022). Finally, this chapter will examine the broader relevance of blockchain analytics to academic research and commercial strategy, emphasizing how transparent, immutable data reshapes everything from compliance protocols to policy-making (Alharby & van Moorsel, 2017; Hewa et al., 2021; Hu et al., 2019). By dissecting these aspects, this chapter aims to provide an in-depth framework for understanding why blockchain analytics has become indispensable in today's rapidly evolving digital ecosystem.

2.2 The Fundamental Nature of Blockchain Analytics

2.2.1 Differences Between Blockchain Analytics and Traditional Data Analysis

Blockchain analytics diverges from traditional data analysis in several key respects. To begin with, data on a blockchain is typically public in the case of permissionless networks like Bitcoin or Ethereum and accessible to anyone with an Internet connection (Casino et al., 2019). Traditional data systems, whether centralized databases or cloud-based repositories, are usually owned by a single entity and protected by various access controls (Tosh et al., 2017; Zyskind et al., 2015). This open access to blockchain data creates both opportunities and challenges. While analysts can tap into large volumes of real-time transaction data without requiring explicit permissions, they must also navigate pseudonymous addresses and cryptographic transactions to extract meaningful insights.

A second critical difference is the immutability and consistency of blockchain data (Yli-Huumo et al., 2016). Once a transaction is recorded and confirmed in a block, altering it becomes prohibitively difficult if not outright impossible on public networks. Traditional data systems, by contrast, allow for updates, deletions, and versioning of records (Elbashir et al., 2008). Such malleability can simplify data governance but also introduces vulnerabilities related to data tampering or data loss. Blockchain's append-only structure requires analytics solutions that can handle cumulative, ever-growing datasets (McConaghy et al., 2016). Analysts often construct data pipelines that continuously monitor new blocks as they are mined or validated, updating internal representations of the ledger state in near real time. This stream-based approach contrasts with static snapshots used in many enterprise data warehouses.

Moreover, the decentralized consensus mechanisms that govern blockchain networks can impact data finality (Bano et al., 2019; Garay & Kiayias, 2020; Wang & Nixon, 2023). Depending on the protocol, there might be a period where recently mined blocks can be reorganized (for example, due to a competing chain in Proof of Work systems) or challenged by validators (in Proof of Stake systems) (Gervais et al., 2014). Analysts must build techniques to handle such eventualities, ensuring that short-term or "probabilistic" data is not treated as definitively final until it has passed a certain number of confirmations. This requirement injects an additional layer of complexity into blockchain analytics pipelines, distinguishing them from more traditional systems where updates in a relational database are usually final the instant they occur.

Finally, blockchain analytics often involves the correlation of on-chain identities with off-chain data (Meiklejohn et al., 2013). In typical enterprise analytics, each data record might be tied to a user ID or a customer profile, easily referencing personal details or purchase histories. Blockchain addresses, by contrast, are pseudonymous strings. While these addresses can be linked to exchanges, smart contracts, or known wallets, they do not directly reveal the identities of their owners. As a result, blockchain analytics frequently entails heuristics, clustering algorithms, or detective work to uncover patterns that might indicate real-world identity or usage. This process raises important questions about privacy, data ethics, and the potential for de-anonymization (Meiklejohn et al., 2013). Hence, blockchain analytics extends beyond pure data crunching, requiring a nuanced understanding of the interplay between cryptographic protocols, economic incentives, and user behaviors in a decentralized environment.

2.2.2 *Impact of Decentralized Structures on Analytical Approaches*

Decentralized architectures have a profound impact on how analysts must approach data collection, storage, and computation. In a traditional client-server model, data is funneled into a central repository, and analysts can apply well-known business intelligence tools or machine learning frameworks to derive insights. With blockchain, data is intrinsically stored across multiple nodes worldwide, each maintaining a copy of the ledger (Monrat et al., 2019; Zheng et al., 2018). Although public data APIs and blockchain explorers provide a simplified interface for retrieving information, these services typically do not offer the full flexibility or granularity needed for advanced analytics. Power users often run their own full nodes, parse the blockchain data independently, and construct specialized indices to query the ledger's historical states or event logs (Soni & Bhushan, 2019; Zou et al., 2020).

This decentralization also influences how computations are performed. On public blockchains, executing computation on-chain can be costly and slow, given the constraints of consensus mechanisms and the need for every node to validate transactions (Lashkari & Musilek, 2021; Wang et al., 2019). Consequently, most in-depth analytics occur off-chain, where data is extracted, transformed, and analyzed using conventional computational resources. However, feeding results back onto the blockchain for subsequent utilization, such as verifying authenticity or triggering automated actions in a smart contract, introduces further design considerations. Protocols seeking to offer advanced analytical features natively may adopt specialized layer-2 scaling solutions, sidechains, or state channels, thereby balancing on-chain transaction finality with off-chain computational efficiency (Gudgeon et al., 2020).

Another dimension to consider is the resilience and fault tolerance of decentralized data. Because blockchain participants can appear and disappear from the network dynamically, analytics strategies must account for data sources that may not always be fully synchronized. Data indexing projects like The Graph or block explorers like Etherscan address this challenge by transforming raw blockchain data into more easily queryable formats (Aimar, 2023; Bai et al., 2020; Khan et al., 2024). Still, analysts remain responsible for validating the reliability of these services. Additionally, decentralized or "multi-chain" ecosystems, in which multiple blockchains interoperate, exacerbate the complexity of data ingestion. Cross-chain bridge transactions, for instance, require the analyst to stitch together transaction flows across different networks, each with its own block times, consensus algorithms, and transaction formats (Han et al., 2023; Mao et al., 2022).

Despite these hurdles, the decentralized nature of blockchain can also yield advantages, such as improved data availability and verifiability (Liu et al., 2023). A well-synced full node ensures that an analyst is working with the exact same dataset as any other participant. This uniformity stands in contrast to traditional data environments, where data discrepancies can occur because of replication lags, partial data sharing, or inconsistent database schemas across organizations (Abadi, 2009).

Blockchain's decentralization thus ensures a single source of cryptographically verified truth, though interpreting that truth effectively remains a sophisticated undertaking (Cachin, 2016).

2.2.3 Multi-Dimensional Analysis: From Transaction Layer to Contract Layer

Blockchain data can be understood through multiple layers, each revealing distinct insights about network activity. At the most fundamental layer, the transaction layer records value transfers between addresses, capturing data points such as sender and recipient addresses, amounts transacted, transaction fees, and timestamps (Agarwal et al., 2024; Wu et al., 2020). Analysts focusing on this layer might examine velocity of funds, identify large transfers that could impact market liquidity, or track suspicious patterns indicative of fraudulent behavior. These transaction-level analyses provide valuable metrics for general network usage, wallet clustering, and even metrics like transaction volume over time (Schnoering & Vazirgiannis, 2025).

Moving up a level, many blockchains, particularly those supporting smart contracts (e.g., Ethereum), introduce a contract execution layer. Here, data includes not only transfers of native tokens but also the invocation of contract-specific methods, logs generated by contract events, and changes in contract state variables (Kell et al., 2024; Tran & Babar, 2020). This layer can be significantly more complex, as contracts can represent a wide variety of functionalities, from decentralized exchanges to gaming platforms, yield farming protocols, or NFT marketplaces (Ortu et al., 2024). Analyzing this layer allows insights into how users interact with specific DApps, how tokens are minted or burned, and how assets move across different contract addresses. DeFi protocols, for instance, produce elaborate transaction patterns involving collateralization, automated market making, and reward distribution (Capponi et al., 2023). Each of these actions leaves a trace in smart contract logs, requiring specialized parsing to convert into interpretable forms like tables of positions, liquidity pools, or token swaps (Kushwaha et al., 2022).

Finally, one can also consider higher-level layers where aggregated behaviors and macro-level trends manifest. This might include dashboards or aggregator services that combine multiple contract-level metrics, providing overviews of network health, DeFi total-value-locked (TVL), or NFT trading volumes across different marketplaces (Tsang et al., 2024). Researchers might then correlate these aggregated metrics with external variables such as macroeconomic indicators or social media sentiment, thus examining how real-world events influence on-chain behaviors, and vice versa (Chalkiadakis et al., 2022). Analyzing the interplay between transaction-level data, contract-level mechanics, and cross-chain metrics offers a holistic perspective that traditional data frameworks rarely achieve (Alamsyah & Muhammad, 2024). In effect, blockchain analytics encompasses every "layer" of the network stack, enabling multi-dimensional insights into user activity, application performance, and systemic health (Glaser, 2017; Kumar et al., 2020).

2.3 The Role of Blockchain Analytics in Academic Research and Business Decision-Making

2.3.1 Strengthening Insights into Decentralized Economic Activities

One of the most compelling advantages of blockchain analytics is its potential to reveal patterns and phenomena in decentralized economic activities that were previously opaque or impossible to study. In traditional economic research, datasets are often derived from surveys, proprietary banking records, or aggregated indices, all of which may be subject to sampling biases or limited accessibility. Blockchains, by contrast, offer an unprecedented level of granularity and completeness: every transaction, contract interaction, and token minting is recorded in a shared ledger, accessible to anyone with the technical means to query it (Casino et al., 2019). This universal accessibility transforms how academics and economists can examine market trends, test hypotheses about behavioral finance, or investigate the impact of monetary policies (e.g., changes in block rewards or protocol-level governance parameters).

A key area of interest lies in the study of network effects and adoption curves. Researchers can observe, in real time, how new protocols gain or lose users, how liquidity pools evolve, and how decentralized governance decisions (like protocol upgrades) influence network participants (Chen & Bellavitis, 2019). Such data-driven insights allow for more robust modeling of how trust, competition, and incentives shape decentralized ecosystems. Moreover, this research extends beyond pure economics to fields such as sociology, political science, and even anthropology, exploring questions of community formation, social capital, and governance structures in digital realms. For instance, the phenomenon of decentralized autonomous organizations (DAOs) can be analyzed by tracking on-chain voting patterns, proposal outcomes, and treasury allocations (Hassan & De Filippi, 2021). These observations yield empirical evidence for theories of collective action, democratized governance, and digital nation-building.

Additionally, from a macro perspective, blockchain analytics grants researchers a lens to explore global financial flows independent of traditional banking rails. Cross-border remittances, peer-to-peer lending, and philanthropic donations can be examined at a granular level, fueling studies that compare transaction fees, adoption rates, and regional preferences (Cermeño, 2016; Lynberg & Deif, 2023). While pseudonymity introduces challenges in attributing real-world identities or geolocations to on-chain addresses, heuristics and external data can partially mitigate these issues. Consequently, a new wave of scholarly work is emerging that leverages on-chain data to address questions about wealth distribution, network centralization vs. decentralization, and the evolution of digital asset markets over time.

2.3.2 *Data Transparency and Traceability as Drivers of New Business Strategies*

From a commercial standpoint, the transparent and traceable nature of blockchain data enables organizations to design innovative business models and competitive strategies. In sectors traditionally plagued by information asymmetry, such as real estate, supply chains, or international remittances, publicly verifiable ledgers can reduce uncertainty and enhance trust among stakeholders. Companies can leverage blockchain analytics to demonstrate compliance, prove solvency, or showcase ethical sourcing practices, thereby attracting customers, partners, or investors who value accountability (Cui et al., 2024). For instance, a fashion brand that sources organic cotton and wants to validate sustainability claims can integrate blockchain-based traceability solutions, then use analytics dashboards to share verifiable supply chain metrics with its customers.

Beyond mere transparency, traceability also opens new revenue streams. Firms can build data products or services that package blockchain-derived insights for other market players (Ofulue & Benyoucef, 2024). Examples include risk scoring systems for decentralized lending platforms, NFT valuation algorithms for collectors, or supply chain optimization modules for logistics providers. Data analytics companies specializing in blockchain often operate on a subscription-based model, offering real-time monitoring, compliance dashboards, or custom data feeds. Additionally, the open nature of blockchain data fosters a vibrant ecosystem of third-party tooling, from analytics libraries to AI-driven insight generators, all feeding on the same underlying source of truth (Zhang & Wen, 2017). This synergy encourages partnerships and cross-pollination, pushing businesses to experiment with new forms of collaboration and value creation.

Moreover, some enterprises are revisiting their organizational and governance structures in light of blockchain's emphasis on decentralization and community-driven decision-making (Beck et al., 2018). Internal analytics teams may evaluate how adopting a token-based loyalty program or implementing a DAO-like structure for shareholder voting could align incentives and spur user engagement (Fromhart & Therattil, 2016). These explorations sometimes culminate in pilot programs or partial migrations to on-chain systems, particularly if analytics indicate strong user adoption or measurable improvements in cost efficiency (Ølnes et al., 2017). Thus, blockchain analytics not only informs day-to-day business operations but can catalyze deeper strategic shifts, fueling innovation in product design, user interaction, and governance models.

2.3.3 *Compliance Audits and Policy-Making*

Lastly, blockchain analytics is integral to compliance audits and policy-making at both corporate and governmental levels. Regulatory agencies worldwide are grappling with how to categorize and oversee blockchain-based activities, from cryptocurrency taxation to securities laws governing token sales (Falk & Hammer, 2023). One major challenge is balancing user privacy rights with the need to monitor illicit activity. Blockchain analytics can offer novel solutions, such as zero-knowledge proofs or "regtech" platforms that allow regulators to verify specific compliance metrics without revealing confidential information (Zhou et al., 2024). However, the more common approach involves analyzing open blockchain data with advanced heuristics and chain-surveillance tools, looking for suspicious patterns that might indicate money laundering or unregistered securities issuance (Sarkar & Das, 2024).

Policymakers can leverage aggregated analytics to gauge the size and growth rate of various blockchain sectors, such as stablecoins or decentralized exchanges, before drafting relevant legislation (Liao & Caramichael, 2022). Tracking real-time data on capital flows and user adoption across jurisdictions can also help policymakers adjust their regulatory approaches promptly, reflecting the dynamic nature of blockchain technology (Adachi et al., 2022). For instance, if certain DeFi platforms gain prominence in enabling cross-border lending, central banks or financial regulatory bodies might need to revise existing frameworks for foreign currency transactions or credit issuance (Gad et al., 2022). In this regard, blockchain analytics can serve as an early warning system, highlighting potential systemic risks or emerging trends.

Similarly, corporate auditors increasingly incorporate blockchain analytics into their methodologies (Bonsón & Bednárová, 2019; Liu et al., 2019). For companies that accept cryptocurrency payments, issue tokens, or hold digital assets on their balance sheets, on-chain transactions must be reconciled with off-chain financial statements (Scharfman, 2022). Auditors can use specialized analytics dashboards to confirm the movement of funds, validate cryptographic signatures, and cross-reference this data with internal accounting records (ALSaqa et al., 2019). This approach reduces the margin of error and helps ensure compliance with evolving accounting standards around digital assets. Over time, as the lines between traditional finance and decentralized models continue to blur, advanced blockchain analytics will be indispensable for integrating on-chain and off-chain records into comprehensive, regulator-approved audits.

2.4 Chapter Conclusion

In sum, this chapter has explored the evolving role of blockchain analytics as a multidisciplinary tool that transcends conventional data analysis frameworks. Rooted in the distinctive properties of decentralized systems with higher transparency, immutability, and pseudonymity level, blockchain analytics requires a rethinking of data collection, processing, and interpretation. Unlike traditional systems, where data is often siloed and editable, blockchain data is distributed, append-only, and publicly accessible, necessitating the use of tailored techniques for querying and parsing. As demonstrated, the analytical process unfolds across multiple layers from transactional flows and contract executions to aggregated cross-chain metrics, each revealing a different dimension of user behavior, protocol logic, and network health.

Furthermore, this chapter highlighted how blockchain analytics serves both academic inquiry and business decision-making. Scholars can now examine economic activity at unprecedented levels of granularity, test behavioral hypotheses, and study governance dynamics in real time. For practitioners, analytics enhances transparency, facilitates compliance, and informs strategic direction, especially in sectors grappling with information asymmetries. The integration of on-chain and off-chain data has proven vital in areas ranging from DeFi risk scoring to supply chain integrity verification.

Finally, as regulation catches up with innovation, the role of blockchain analytics in supporting compliance audits and shaping policy frameworks becomes increasingly prominent. From regtech tools to chain surveillance systems, analytics is a cornerstone of both oversight and enforcement. Looking ahead, paired with rising data complexity, the continued expansion of blockchain use cases will only deepen the need for advanced analytical infrastructure. Thus, blockchain analytics stands not only as a technical competency but as a foundational layer in the architecture of decentralized systems, shaping how knowledge is produced, verified, and acted upon in the digital economy.

References

Abadi, D. J. (2009). Data management in the cloud: Limitations and opportunities. *The Bulletin of the Technical Committee on Data Engineering, 32*(1), 3–12.

Adachi, M., et al. (2022). 'Stablecoins' role in crypto and beyond: functions, risks and policy. *Macroprudential Bulletin, 18*. Retrieved April 3, 2025, from https://ideas.repec.org/a/ecb/ecbmbu/202200182.html

Agarwal, U., et al. (2024). Blockchain and crypto forensics: Investigating crypto frauds. *International Journal of Network Management, 34*(2), e2255. https://doi.org/10.1002/nem.2255

Aimar, D. (2023). *Extraction, indexing and analysis of Ethereum smart contracts data*. PhD Thesis. Politecnico di Torino. Retrieved April 3, 2025, from https://webthesis.biblio.polito.it/28450/

Alamsyah, A., & Muhammad, I. F. (2024). Unraveling the crypto market: A journey into decentralized finance transaction network. *Digital Business, 4*(1), 100074. https://doi.org/10.1016/j.digbus.2024.100074

Alharby, M., & van Moorsel, A. (2017). Blockchain-based smart contracts: A systematic mapping study. *Computer Science & Information Technology (CS & IT)*, 125–140. https://doi.org/10.5121/csit.2017.71011

Alqassem, I., Rahwan, I., & Svetinovic, D. (2020). The anti-social system properties: Bitcoin network data analysis. *IEEE Transactions on Systems, Man, and Cybernetics: Systems, 50*(1), 21–31. https://doi.org/10.1109/TSMC.2018.2883678

ALSaqa, Z. H., Hussein, A. I., & Mahmood, S. M. (2019). The impact of blockchain on accounting information systems. *Journal of Information Technology Management, 11*(3), 62–80.

Ante, L. (2022). The non-fungible token (NFT) market and its relationship with bitcoin and Ethereum. *FinTech, 1*(3), 216–224. https://doi.org/10.3390/fintech1030017

Ante, L. (2023). Non-fungible token (NFT) markets on the Ethereum blockchain: Temporal development, cointegration and interrelations. *Economics of Innovation and New Technology, 32*(8), 1216–1234. https://doi.org/10.1080/10438599.2022.2119564

Bai, Q., et al. (2020). *Evolution of ethereum: A temporal graph perspective*. arXiv. https://doi.org/10.48550/arXiv.2001.05251

Bano, S., et al. (2019). SoK: Consensus in the age of blockchains. In *Proceedings of the 1st ACM conference on advances in financial technologies. AFT'19: 1st ACM conference on advances in financial technologies* (pp. 183–198). ACM. https://doi.org/10.1145/3318041.3355458

Bartoletti, M., et al. (2017). A general framework for blockchain analytics. In *Proceedings of the 1st workshop on scalable and resilient infrastructures for distributed ledgers* (pp. 1–6). Association for Computing Machinery (SERIAL'17). https://doi.org/10.1145/3152824.3152831

Beck, R., Müller-Bloch, C., & King, J. L. (2018). Governance in the blockchain economy: A framework and research agenda. *Journal of the Association for Information Systems, 19*(10), 1.

Bonsón, E., & Bednárová, M. (2019). Blockchain and its implications for accounting and auditing. *Meditari Accountancy Research, 27*(5), 725–740.

Cachin, C. (2016). Architecture of the hyperledger blockchain fabric. In *Workshop on distributed cryptocurrencies and consensus ledgers*. Chicago, IL (pp. 1–4). Retrieved April 3, 2025, from https://cognizium.io/uploads/resources/IBM%20Research%20-%20Architecture%20of%20the%20Hyperledger%20Blockchain%20Fabric%20-%202016%20-%20July.pdf

Cai, T., et al. (2023). On-chain and off-chain scalability techniques. In W. Chen, Z. Zheng, & H. Huang (Eds.), *Blockchain scalability* (pp. 81–96). Springer Nature. https://doi.org/10.1007/978-981-99-1059-5_3

Capponi, A., Iyengar, G., & Sethuraman, J. (2023). Decentralized finance: Protocols, risks, and governance. *Foundations and Trends® in Privacy and Security, 5*(3), 144–188.

Carapella, F., et al. (2022). *Decentralized finance (DeFi): Transformative potential and associated risks*. https://doi.org/10.2139/ssrn.5191051

Casino, F., Dasaklis, T. K., & Patsakis, C. (2019). A systematic literature review of blockchain-based applications: Current status, classification and open issues. *Telematics and Informatics, 36*, 55–81. https://doi.org/10.1016/j.tele.2018.11.006

Cermeño, J.S. (2016). *Blockchain in financial services: Regulatory landscape and future challenges for its commercial application*. BBVA Research Madrid, Spain. Retrieved April 3, 2025, from https://www.smallake.kr/wp-content/uploads/2017/01/WP_16-20.pdf

Chalkiadakis, I., et al. (2022). On-chain analytics for sentiment-driven statistical causality in cryptocurrencies. *Blockchain: Research and Applications, 3*(2), 100063. https://doi.org/10.1016/j.bcra.2022.100063

Chen, Y., & Bellavitis, C. (2019). Decentralized finance: Blockchain technology and the quest for an open financial system, *Stevens Institute of Technology School of Business Research Paper* [Preprint]. Retrieved April 3, 2025, from https://www.researchgate.net/profile/Yan-Chen-30/publication/334658377_Decentralized_Finance_Blockchain_Technology_and_the_Quest_for_an_Open_Financial_System/links/6526dbd082fd2a6bab872831/Decentralized-Finance-Blockchain-Technology-and-the-Quest-for-an-Open-Financial-System.pdf

Cui, Y., Gaur, V., & Liu, J. (2024). Supply chain transparency and blockchain design. *Management Science, 70*(5), 3245–3263. https://doi.org/10.1287/mnsc.2023.4851

Elbashir, M. Z., Collier, P. A., & Davern, M. J. (2008). Measuring the effects of business intelligence systems: The relationship between business process and organizational performance.

International Journal of Accounting Information Systems, 9(3), 135–153. https://doi.org/10.1016/j.accinf.2008.03.001

Falk, B. H., & Hammer, S. (2023). A comprehensive approach to crypto regulation. *U. Pa. J. Bus. L., 25*, 415.

Feltovic, M. (2024). Utilizing blockchain technology to modernize police operations: ensuring security, transparency, and efficiency. *Eximia, 13*, 661–672. https://doi.org/10.47577/eximia.v13i1.493

Fromhart, S., & Therattil, L. (2016). *Making blockchain real for customer loyalty rewards programs*. Deloitte Development LLC [Preprint].

Gad, A. G., et al. (2022). Emerging trends in blockchain technology and applications: A review and outlook. *Journal of King Saud University, Computer and Information Sciences, 34*(9), 6719–6742. https://doi.org/10.1016/j.jksuci.2022.03.007

Garay, J., & Kiayias, A. (2020). SoK: A consensus taxonomy in the blockchain era. In S. Jarecki (Ed.), *Topics in cryptology—CT-RSA 2020* (Lecture notes in computer science) (pp. 284–318). Springer International Publishing. https://doi.org/10.1007/978-3-030-40186-3_13

Gervais, A., et al. (2014). Is bitcoin a decentralized currency? *IEEE Security and Privacy, 12*(3), 54–60.

Glaser, F. (2017). Pervasive decentralisation of digital infrastructures: A framework for blockchain enabled system and use case analysis. In *Hawaii International Conference on System Sciences 2017 (HICSS-50)* [Preprint]. https://aisel.aisnet.org/hicss-50/da/open_digital_services/4

Gudgeon, L., et al. (2020). SoK: Layer-two blockchain protocols. In J. Bonneau & N. Heninger (Eds.), *Financial cryptography and data security* (Lecture notes in computer science) (pp. 201–226). Springer International Publishing. https://doi.org/10.1007/978-3-030-51280-4_12

Gunay, S., & Kaskaloglu, K. (2022). Does utilizing smart contracts induce a financial connectedness between Ethereum and non-fungible tokens? *Research in International Business and Finance, 63*, 101773. https://doi.org/10.1016/j.ribaf.2022.101773

Han, P., et al. (2023). A survey on cross-chain technologies. *Distributed Ledger Technologies: Research and Practice, 2*(2), 1–30. https://doi.org/10.1145/3573896

Hassan, S., & De Filippi, P. (2021). Decentralized autonomous organization. *Internet Policy Review, 10*(2). Retrieved April 3, 2025, from https://policyreview.info/pdf/policyreview-2021-2-1556.pdf

Hellani, H., et al. (2021). On blockchain integration with supply chain: Overview on data transparency. *Logistics, 5*(3), 46. https://doi.org/10.3390/logistics5030046

Hepp, T., et al. (2018). On-chain vs. off-chain storage for supply-and blockchain integration. *IT—Information Technology, 60*(5–6), 283–291. https://doi.org/10.1515/itit-2018-0019

Hewa, T. M., et al. (2021). Survey on blockchain-based smart contracts: Technical aspects and future research. *IEEEAccess, 9*, 87643–87662. https://doi.org/10.1109/ACCESS.2021.3068178

Hu, Y., et al. (2019). *Blockchain-based smart contracts—applications and challenges*. arXiv. https://doi.org/10.48550/arXiv.1810.04699

Kaplanov, N. (2012). Nerdy money: Bitcoin, the private digital currency, and the case against its regulation student article. *Loyola Consumer Law Review, 25*(1), 111–174.

Kell, T., et al. (2024). Forsage: Anatomy of a smart-contract pyramid scheme. In F. Baldimtsi & C. Cachin (Eds.), *Financial cryptography and data security* (Lecture notes in computer science) (pp. 241–258). Springer Nature. https://doi.org/10.1007/978-3-031-47751-5_14

Khan, B. U. I., et al. (2024). A scalability enhancement scheme for Ethereum Blockchains: A graph-based decentralized approach. *Engineering, Technology & Applied Science Research, 14*(6), 17725–17736.

Kumar, K. S., et al. (2020). Blockchain technology: an insight into architecture, use cases, and its application with industrial IoT and big data. In *Blockchain technology* (pp. 23–42). CRC Press. Retrieved April 3, 2025, from https://www.taylorfrancis.com/chapters/edit/10.1201/9781003004998-3/blockchain-technology-suresh-kumar-ananth-kumar-radhamani-sundaresan

Kushwaha, S. S., et al. (2022). Ethereum smart contract analysis tools: A systematic review. *IEEE Access, 10*, 57037–57062.
Kuzuno, H., & Karam, C. (2017). Blockchain explorer: An analytical process and investigation environment for bitcoin. In *2017 APWG Symposium on Electronic Crime Research (eCrime)* (pp. 9–16). https://doi.org/10.1109/ECRIME.2017.7945049
Lashkari, B., & Musilek, P. (2021). A comprehensive review of blockchain consensus mechanisms. *IEEE Access, 9*, 43620–43652.
Liao, G.Y., & Caramichael, J. (2022). *Stablecoins: Growth potential and impact on banking*. Retrieved April 3, 2025, from https://www.federalreserve.gov/econres/ifdp/stablecoins-growth-potential-and-impact-on-banking.htm?utm_source=in_materials
Liu, M., Wu, K., & Xu, J. J. (2019). How will blockchain technology impact auditing and accounting: Permissionless versus permissioned blockchain. *Current Issues in Auditing, 13*(2), A19–A29.
Liu, X., et al. (2023). Blockchain data availability scheme with strong data privacy protection. *Information, 14*(2), 88.
Lynberg, L., & Deif, A. (2023). Network effects in blockchain and supply chain: a theoretical research synthesis. *Modern Supply Chain Research and Applications, 5*(1), 2–27. https://doi.org/10.1108/MSCRA-07-2022-0016
Mafrur, R. (2025) *Blockchain data analytics: Review and challenges*. arXiv. https://doi.org/10.48550/arXiv.2503.09165
Mao, H., et al. (2022). A survey on cross-chain technology: Challenges, development, and prospect. *IEEE Access, 11*, 45527–45546.
McConaghy, T., et al. (2016). Bigchaindb: A scalable blockchain database. In *White Paper, BigChainDB* (pp. 53–72).
McGinn, D., McIlwraith, D., & Guo, Y. (2018). Towards open data blockchain analytics: a bitcoin perspective. *Royal Society Open Science, 5*(8), 180298. https://doi.org/10.1098/rsos.180298
Meiklejohn, S., et al. (2013). A fistful of bitcoins: characterizing payments among men with no names. In *Proceedings of the 2013 conference on internet measurement conference. IMC'13: Internet measurement conference* (pp. 127–140). Barcelona, ACM. https://doi.org/10.1145/2504730.2504747
Monrat, A. A., Schelén, O., & Andersson, K. (2019). A survey of blockchain from the perspectives of applications, challenges, and opportunities. *IEEE Access, 7*, 117134–117151.
Ofulue, J., & Benyoucef, M. (2024). Data monetization: insights from a technology-enabled literature review and research agenda. *Management Review Quarterly, 74*(2), 521–565. https://doi.org/10.1007/s11301-022-00309-1
Ølnes, S., Ubacht, J., & Janssen, M. (2017) Blockchain in government: Benefits and implications of distributed ledger technology for information sharing. In *Government information quarterly*. Elsevier. Retrieved April 3, 2025, from https://www.sciencedirect.com/science/article/pii/S0740624X17303155?casa_token=Hc_J6YLi03AAAAAA:3-LK5ix3n_sGrTFYifK_cxL-DugGDYveEA_CzbuR8YWQkilZvCoCRtwMlRd-XrF9gZUPBQQ5D
Ortu, M., et al. (2024). Taxonomic insights into ethereum smart contracts by linking application categories to security vulnerabilities. *Scientific Reports, 14*(1), 23433.
Sarkar, A. K., & Das, A. (2024). Deep enhancement in Supplychain management with adaptive Serial cascaded autoencoder with long short term memory and multi-layered perceptron framework. *Annals of Data Science, 12*(5), 1–30.
Scharfman, J. (2022). Compliance and governance for crypto-asset managers, in Scharfman, J., Cryptocurrency compliance and operations. : Springer International Publishing, pp. 73–89. https://doi.org/10.1007/978-3-030-88000-2_4
Schnoering, H., & Vazirgiannis, M. (2025). Bitcoin research with a transaction graph dataset. *Scientific Data, 12*(1), 404.
Schueffel, P. (2021). DeFi: Decentralized finance—An introduction and overview. *Journal of Innovation Management, 9*(3), I–XI. https://doi.org/10.24840/2183-0606_009.003_0001

Sharma, A., et al. (2022). Bitcoin's Blockchain data analytics: A graph theoretic perspective. In L. Barolli, F. Hussain, & T. Enokido (Eds.), *Advanced information networking and applications* (pp. 459–470). Springer International Publishing. https://doi.org/10.1007/978-3-030-99584-3_40

Soni, S., & Bhushan, B. (2019). A comprehensive survey on blockchain: Working, security analysis, privacy threats and potential applications. In *2019 2nd international conference on intelligent computing, instrumentation and control technologies (ICICICT)* (pp. 922–926). IEEE. Retrieved April 3, 2025, from https://ieeexplore.ieee.org/abstract/document/8993210/

Tosh, D. K., et al. (2017). Security implications of blockchain cloud with analysis of block withholding attack. In *2017 17th IEEE/ACM international symposium on cluster, cloud and grid computing (CCGRID)* (pp. 458–467). https://doi.org/10.1109/CCGRID.2017.111

Tran, N.K., & Babar, M.A. (2020). Anatomy, concept, and design space of blockchain networks. In *2020 IEEE international conference on software architecture (ICSA)* (pp. 125–134). IEEE. Retrieved April 3, 2025, from https://ieeexplore.ieee.org/abstract/document/9101315/

Tsang, Y. P., et al. (2024). On-chain and off-chain data management for blockchain-Internet of Things: A multi-agent deep reinforcement learning approach. *Journal of Grid Computing, 22*(1), 16. https://doi.org/10.1007/s10723-023-09739-x

Wang, G., & Nixon, M. (2023). SoK: Essentials of BFT consensus for blockchains. In *2023 fifth international conference on blockchain computing and applications (BCCA)* (pp. 315–328). IEEE. Retrieved April 3, 2025, from https://ieeexplore.ieee.org/abstract/document/10338868/

Wang, W., et al. (2019). A survey on consensus mechanisms and mining strategy management in blockchain networks. *IEEE Access, 7*, 22328–22370.

Wu, Y., et al. (2020). A bitcoin transaction network analytic method for future blockchain forensic investigation. *IEEE Transactions on Network Science and Engineering, 8*(2), 1230–1241.

Xu, Q., et al. (2018). A blockchain-based storage system for data analytics in the internet of things. In R. R. Yager & J. Pascual Espada (Eds.), *New advances in the internet of things* (pp. 119–138). Springer International Publishing. https://doi.org/10.1007/978-3-319-58190-3_8

Yli-Huumo, J., et al. (2016). Where is current research on blockchain technology?—A systematic review. *PLoS One, 11*(10), e0163477. https://doi.org/10.1371/journal.pone.0163477

Zhang, Y., & Wen, J. (2017). The IoT electric business model: Using blockchain technology for the internet of things. *Peer-to-Peer Networking and Applications, 10*, 983–994.

Zheng, Z., et al. (2018). Blockchain challenges and opportunities: a survey. *International Journal of Web and Grid Services, 14*(4), 352. https://doi.org/10.1504/IJWGS.2018.095647

Zhou, L., et al. (2024). Leveraging zero knowledge proofs for blockchain-based identity sharing: A survey of advancements, challenges and opportunities. *Journal of Information Security and Applications, 80*, 103678. https://doi.org/10.1016/j.jisa.2023.103678

Zou, Y., et al. (2020). Focus on blockchain: A comprehensive survey on academic and application. *IEEE Access, 8*, 187182–187201.

Zyskind, G., Nathan, O., & Pentland, A. S. (2015). Decentralizing privacy: Using blockchain to protect personal data. In *2015 IEEE security and privacy workshops* (pp. 180–184). https://doi.org/10.1109/SPW.2015.27

Tao Tang is a leading expert in digital transformation, natural language processing (NLP), and AI-driven financial analytics. He now serves as AI and Web 3 engineer at the University of Surrey. His research focuses on leveraging machine learning and NLP techniques to extract and analyze unstructured data from global publicly listed companies. With a strong publication record in top-tier journals and presentations at major international conferences, Dr. Tang's work offers valuable insights into the effective adoption and impact of AI and digital technologies in modern business practices.

Chapter 3
Blockchain-Powered DeFi: Exploring Adoption Drivers and Risk Challenges

Amit Kumar Jaiswal

3.1 Introduction

Decentralized Finance (DeFi) is a blockchain-based financial system that eliminates intermediaries such as banks, relying instead on a peer-to-peer network of validators to execute transactions securely. Blockchains such as Ethereum are permissionless, allowing anyone to participate as a user or validator without registration. This makes DeFi a permissionless financial ecosystem where anyone can offer or use services. However, the lack of identity verification means laws and regulations can often be bypassed, though this does not imply legality in all jurisdictions. Blockchain and DeFi are studied due to their widespread use, not their inherent merits or drawbacks. As of March 2025, DeFi's total value locked (TVL)[1] has surged to approximately $92.5 billion up from $54.2 billion earlier in the year, a 75% year-to-date increase.[2] Whether seen as revolutionary or controversial, DeFi's growing adoption across finance, technology, and other sectors underscores its significance as a subject for academic research. Some of the key aspects of blockchain and DeFi, (a) ERC-20 tokens, which have become integral to DeFi ecosystems (see Fig. 3.1), and (b) leveraged tokens (LVTs) as extension of ERC-20 tokens which provide traders with amplified exposure but come with inherent risks. ERC-20 tokens play a pivotal role in enhancing the functionality of the Ethereum blockchain and decentralized

[1] https://defillama.com

[2] https://www.binance.com/en/blog/crypto/key-trends-in-crypto-october-2024

A. K. Jaiswal (✉)
Endless Protocol, Guildford, UK

University of Surrey, Guildford, UK

Indian Institute of Technology (BHU) Varanasi, Varanasi, India
e-mail: amit@endless.link; a.jaiswal@surrey.ac.uk; amit.chr@iitbhu.ac.in

Y. Xiong (ed.), *Blockchain Analytics for Practitioners*, Business Analytics in Practice, https://doi.org/10.1007/978-3-032-06046-4_3

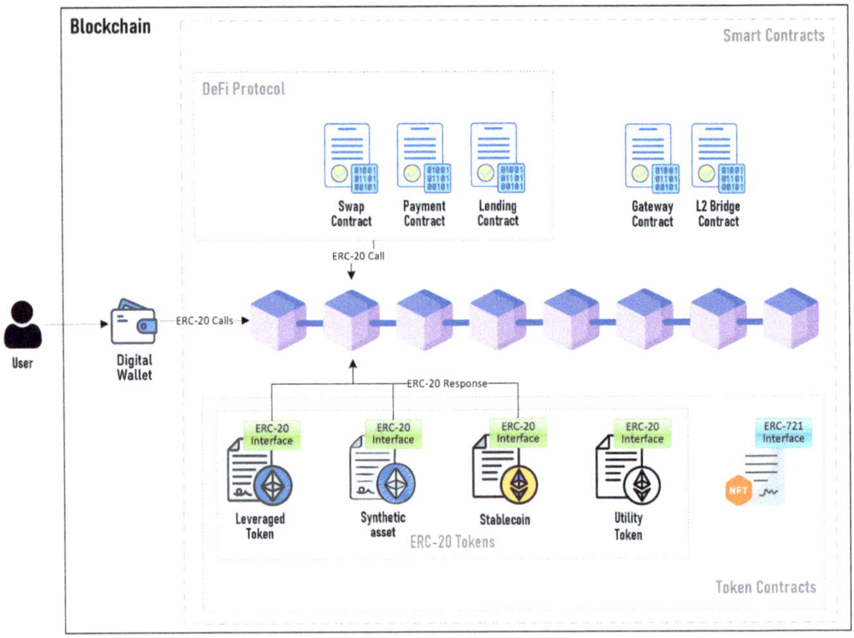

Fig. 3.1 The Ethereum and DeFi ecosystem is anchored by the Ethereum Blockchain layer, which enables smart contract functionality. Within this ecosystem, ERC-20 tokens—categorized as leveraged tokens, stablecoins, and utility tokens—play a central role. These tokens interface with DeFi protocols, including lending platforms and decentralized exchanges, primarily adhering to the ERC-20 standard for fungible token interactions

finance. Among the various core aspects of blockchain technology, ERC-20 tokens are particularly useful due to their foundational importance in DeFi ecosystems. They serve as the primary framework for asset tokenization enabling the creation of stablecoins, governance tokens, and utility tokens, which are integral to nearly all decentralized applications (dApps). Also, ERC-20 tokens underpin essential DeFi mechanisms including liquidity pools, lending protocols, decentralized exchanges, and governance systems. ERC-20 tokens are smart contracts adhering to a standardized interface, which specifies rules and functions to ensure interoperability with other smart contracts and decentralized applications. However, as all programming languages, they are susceptible to security vulnerabilities. Analyzing ERC-20 tokens provides critical insights into the mechanisms of decentralized asset representation and transfer, essential for improving their security. We highlight insights into the security challenges of ERC-20 tokens to identify potential improvements and ensure adherence to best practices. By addressing these vulnerabilities, it can enhance the security of ERC-20 tokens, solidifying their foundational role in the decentralized finance ecosystem. Leveraged tokens (LVTs) unlike ERC-20 tokens are not a core component of blockchain infrastructure but introduce significant complexity warranting academic exploration. While LVTs attract users with the

Table 3.1 Protection mechanisms for users holding ERC-20 tokens or LVTs

Risk to users	Technical reason	Protection mechanism
Inability to custody Transparency in total supply Transparency in transactions Transparency in token holders interoperability with DeFi Challenges in auditing Inadequate financial backing	Assets are locked in the exchange Total supply are not published transaction are not publicly disclosed Ownership is confidential Token works in isolation Code of the token is not public Futures issued after the launch of the token	Implementation on the blockchain
Possibility of front-running	Exploited fund trade during well-known events	Randomized rebalancing or iceberg orders
Higher tracking error	Inefficient rebalancing algorithm	Optimization of rebalancing algorithms
Higher management fees	Inefficient cost management	Cross-trading or implementation on layer 2 chains
Multiple withdrawal attack	Withdraw from user wallet more than approved	Securing transferFrom method

potential for amplified returns, many lack a thorough understanding of their technical intricacies, such as volatility decay, rebalancing mechanisms, and adverse market impacts. This knowledge gap often leads to misjudgments, where users overestimate potential gains or underestimate loss exposure. Researching LVTs aims to clarify these mechanisms (see Table 3.1), enhancing comprehension for developers and users while mitigating associated risks.

3.2 The Web of Trust: Blockchain's Unfolding Potential

Blockchain technology is characterized by its decentralized and permissionless network architecture, enabling dynamic participation of nodes without reliance on a central authority. Data integrity is maintained through distributed consensus mechanisms, such as Proof of Work or Proof of Stake, ensuring resilience against individual node failures. This inherent fault tolerance allows for continuous operation despite hardware or communication disruptions, as each node maintains a consistent replica of the data ledger. Beyond its technical robustness, the blockchain market has exhibited substantial growth. Industry analyses indicate an average annual growth rate of 51% from 2016 to 2022, culminating in revenues exceeding $2 billion USD by 2022 (Stamford, 2019; Reportlinker, 2020). Projections suggest continued expansion, with the global market anticipated to reach $39.7 billion by 2025, reflecting a 67.3% annual growth rate (Grand View Research, 2020). The financial services sector is at the forefront of blockchain adoption, with widespread integration into payment and settlement systems anticipated. Furthermore, the decentralized finance ecosystem has experienced exponential growth, evidenced by a total value locked surpassing $200 billion in 2021 (MarketsandMarkets, 2020), demonstrating the technology's efficacy in facilitating peer-to-peer lending, borrowing, and trading. The utility of blockchain extends beyond finance, with significant adoption projected in healthcare for secure patient record management, with an estimated 55% integration by 2025 (Labs, 2020). Supply chain management is another rapidly integrating sector, leveraging blockchain for enhanced transparency and traceability, as exemplified by implementations at companies such as Walmart and IBM (Sristy, 2021).

3.2.1 Smart Contract Ecosystem

Amongst a diverse array of blockchain implementations, numbering 22 according to recent surveys,[3] Ethereum (Wood et al., 2014) has achieved significant industrial adoption. Launched in 2015, following its initial proposal in 2013, Ethereum currently holds the second-largest market capitalization. Its robust development community actively contributes to its evolution through the proposal and tracking of enhancements.[4] Ethereum facilitates the deployment and execution of decentralized applications on its blockchain platform. A core component of Ethereum's architecture is the smart contract, which has gained widespread acceptance, evidenced by the substantial volume of digital assets, including ETH, ERC-20 tokens, digital wallets, and DeFi protocols, managed within its ecosystem. Smart contracts are decentralized executable programs whose operational logic is embedded within their code, thereby enforcing predefined rules. These contracts execute autonomously, eliminating the need for third-party intermediaries, thus enhancing transparency and mitigating manipulation risks. Within the Ethereum environment, smart contracts are deployed on-chain, achieving immutability and tamper-proof status upon publication. Developers utilize high-level programming languages such as Solidity and Vyper to create these contracts, enabling a range of functionalities from simple token transfers to complex dApp interactions. The programmability of smart contracts allows for the implementation of diverse mechanisms, including token exchanges, voting systems, and multi-signature wallets, effectively forming the foundational infrastructure of Ethereum's functionality. However, as with any emerging technology, security remains a critical concern for smart contracts. Previous research has indicated that approximately 45% of deployed Ethereum smart contracts exhibit vulnerabilities (Luu et al., 2016). The complexity of smart contract development has been demonstrated to be error-prone, resulting in the prevalence of security flaws. A prominent example is the 2016 TheDAO exploit,

[3] https://builtin.com/blockchain/blockchain-platforms

[4] https://www.coindesk.com/coindesk20

which resulted in a loss of 60 million US dollars (Siegel, 2016). Analogous to traditional programming languages, smart contract code is susceptible to exploitation by adversaries, including miners, external users, and other contracts, for malicious manipulation and financial gain. The substantial financial value held within some smart contracts serves as a significant incentive for such adversarial activities.

Example 1 Decentralized finance platforms have demonstrated significant growth and adoption. Aave, a prominent decentralized lending protocol, consistently maintains a total value locked exceeding $6 billion. This platform facilitates interest accrual for users who supply digital assets and enables the acquisition of loans through the provision of cryptocurrency deposits as collateral. Similarly, Uniswap, a leading decentralized exchange (DEX), exhibits a TVL of approximately $3.7 billion. This platform empowers users to execute direct cryptocurrency trades from their personal digital wallets (Block, 2024).

3.3 Decentralized Applications and ERC-20 Tokens

The migration of applications from centralized to decentralized architectures offers potential solutions to critical challenges, including single points of failure, hardware and maintenance expenditures, and data security. These decentralized applications operate across untrusted networks and utilize smart contracts for on-blockchain code execution. Given the substantial market capitalization of many tokens, a subset of smart contracts, security is paramount. Furthermore, the holding of tokens by commercial entities, which are often subject to financial auditing requirements, necessitates the verification of the underlying smart contract's correctness by professional auditors. Ethereum enables dApps to both utilize its native cryptocurrency, ETH, and issue custom tokens for diverse purposes, such as in-application purchases, interoperability with other dApps, and the representation of digital assets. These tokens may function as alternative currencies with distinct properties, serve as access credentials for dApp functionalities, or represent ownership of off-chain assets. Interoperability with other dApps and off-blockchain web applications, such as exchange services, is a desirable feature. To facilitate this, the Ethereum community has adopted the ERC-20 token standard (Fabian Vogelsteller, 2015). As illustrated in Fig. 3.2, ERC-20 defines an interface comprising abstract methods, including their names, parameters, and return types, and provides implementation guidelines. However, it does not offer a concrete implementation. Developers retain the flexibility to implement ERC-20 methods according to the specific requirements of their dApps, and even to extend the standard with novel functionalities, such as leveraged tokens.

Despite the proliferation of alternative token standards, including ERC-721, ERC-777, and ERC-1155, among others, the ERC-20 standard maintains its pre-eminence within the Ethereum ecosystem. Analysis of the approximately 2.5 million smart contracts deployed on the Ethereum network reveals that approximately

```
contract ERC20Interface {
    function totalSupply() external view returns (uint256);
    function balanceOf(address _account) external view returns (uint256);
    function transfer(address _to, uint256 _tokens) external returns (bool);
    function approve(address _spender, uint256 _tokens) external returns (bool);
    function transferFrom(address _from, address _to, uint256 _tokens) external returns (bool);
    function allowance(address _account, address _spender) external view returns (uint256);

    event Transfer(address indexed _from, address indexed _to, uint256 _tokens);
    event Approval(address indexed _tokenOwner, address indexed _spender, uint256 _tokens);
}
```

Fig. 3.2 Within the Solidity programming environment, the ERC-20 interface establishes a defined set of functional requirements that must be satisfied by any contract seeking ERC-20 compliance. The fulfillment of these requirements is essential for enabling seamless interaction and compatibility with other components of the ERC-20 ecosystem, including wallets, exchanges, and decentralized applications

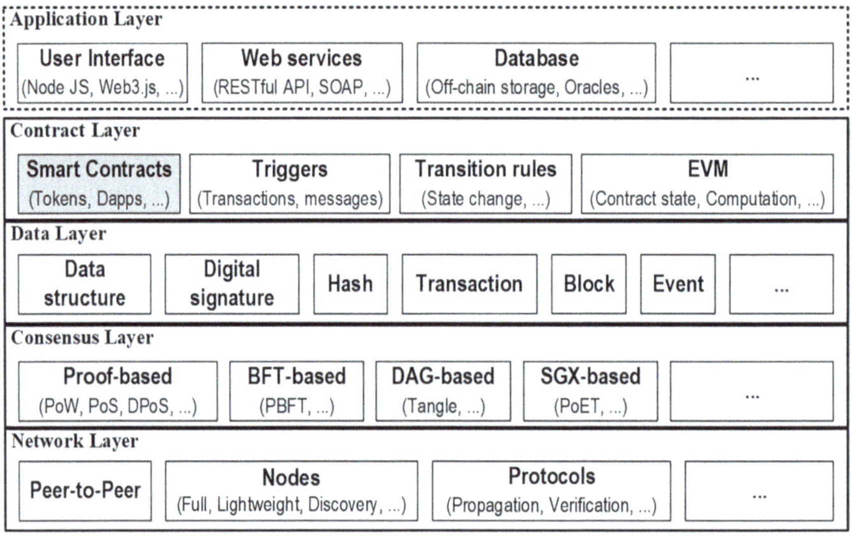

Fig. 3.3 Smart contracts operate within the contract layer, a specialized component of the application layer, wherein they harness the security afforded by the underlying consensus mechanisms for reliable execution and state modification. This layer is dedicated to the operational dynamics of smart contracts and their interaction with blockchain transactions

260,000 are token contracts. Also, 98% of these token contracts adhere to the ERC-20 standard (Tracker, 2020), underscoring its pervasive adoption across industry stakeholders, smart contract developers, and the broader Ethereum community. As illustrated in Fig. 3.3, within the hierarchical architecture of the Ethereum blockchain, ERC-20 tokens reside within the Contract layer, which serves as the execution environment for dApp back-end logic.

3.4 Tokens and Leveraged Exchange-Traded Fund

Exchange-Traded Funds (ETFs) are structured as weighted portfolios of equities, selected based on shared characteristics, such as sector affiliation or market capitalization. These portfolios are subsequently divided into shares, which are then traded on public exchanges, mirroring the trading mechanisms of individual stocks (Liebi, 2020).

Example 2 The *Direxion Daily S&P500 Bull 3x ETF (SPXL)* is a leveraged exchange-traded fund designed to provide a daily return three times that of the S&P500 index. Specifically, it aims to amplify each 1% daily movement in the S&P500 index to a corresponding 3% movement, whether positive or negative. Conversely, the *Direxion Daily S&P500 Bear 3x ETF (SPXS)* is engineered to deliver a daily return that is three times the inverse of the S&P500 index's performance. Consequently, a 1% daily decline in the S&P500 index results in a 3% daily gain for SPXS, and vice versa (Wided, 2019; Lettau & Madhavan, 2018).

Leveraged ETFs (LETFs) introduced in 2006 are designed to provide amplified daily returns relative to their underlying asset portfolios. Specifically, LETFs aim to achieve a multiple of the daily performance of the underlying asset. Conversely, inverse LETFs seek to deliver a return that is a multiple of the inverse of the underlying asset's daily performance (Hill & Foster, 2009; Cheng & Madhavan, 2009; Securities & Commission, 2023). In common investor parlance, LETFs and inverse LETFs are frequently referred to as "bullish" and "bearish" ETFs, respectively, reflecting the short-term directional expectations of market participants regarding future price movements.

Leveraged Tokens (LVTs) can be conceptualized as the cryptocurrency and cryptoasset ("crypto") market's analog to Leveraged Exchange-Traded Funds. Mirroring the function of LETFs, LVTs utilize leveraged instruments within the crypto market to achieve daily returns that exceed those of the underlying asset. While LETFs predominantly employ active management strategies, LVTs are characterized by three distinct management paradigms, centralized, decentralized, and hybrid. Centralized LVTs are primarily administered by cryptocurrency exchanges, facilitating acquisition via spot market transactions, akin to conventional cryptocurrency purchases, or directly from the issuing entity. Decentralized LVTs, conversely, operate on the blockchain through ERC-20 smart contracts, enabling peer-to-peer trading without reliance on intermediaries. Hybrid LVTs represent a confluence of these models, embodying decentralized LVT functionalities while being traded on centralized cryptocurrency exchanges. The adoption of centralized exchanges is often driven by user preferences for intuitive interfaces, continuous-time order book mechanisms (as opposed to automated market makers, which are the predominant on-chain trading mechanism), and enhanced liquidity through the aggregation of buy and sell orders. However, this hybrid approach introduces inherent disadvantages stemming from the integration of centralized and decentralized systems, including, but not limited to, functional complexities, security vulnerabilities, and custodial risks.

Example 3 Issuers may introduce LVTs, exemplified by BTC3L and BTC3S, which track the performance of Bitcoin (BTC) as the underlying asset. These LVTs utilize Bitcoin perpetual futures contracts (BTC-Perp) as the leveraged instrument, aiming to amplify short-term Bitcoin price fluctuations. The numerical prefix "3" in the LVT nomenclature denotes the leverage multiplier, indicating a triple-leveraged position, while the suffix "L" or "S" signifies a long or short market exposure, respectively. Specifically, BTC3L is designed to yield a 3% gain for each 1% increase in the Bitcoin price, and conversely, a 3% loss for each 1% decrease. In contrast, BTC3S is configured to generate a 3% gain when the Bitcoin price declines by 1%, and a corresponding 3% loss when the price ascends by 1%.

3.4.1 Compounding Effect in LVTs

Volatility, in financial contexts, quantifies the rate of fluctuation in an asset's value. Assets exhibiting high volatility demonstrate a wider range of potential values and are prone to rapid, substantial price variations in either direction. Conversely, low-volatility assets maintain relatively stable prices with minimal fluctuations. For instance, within equity markets, a stock is deemed volatile when its price experiences sustained movements exceeding a 1% threshold, particularly when compared to its historical price data (Hayes, 2023). This deviation from historical norms signifies a heightened degree of price variability and consequently increased volatility.

3.4.2 Leverage Products

LVTs derive their valuation from a leveraged fund, which itself is predicated upon a leveraged product. As depicted in Fig. 3.4, these leveraged products typically originate from either the cryptocurrency derivatives market or the decentralized finance (DeFi) lending market. Within the derivatives market, perpetual futures (perps) have gained prominence due to their inherent flexibility. The absence of an expiration date in perps facilitates indefinite holding periods, offering the supplementary benefit of establishing leveraged positions in LVTs without the associated risks of contract expiration or rollover.

Conversely, the DeFi lending market presents a comparatively conservative alternative. This market enables LVTs to secure asset loans through decentralized platforms such as Aave and Compound. While perpetual futures allow for higher leverage and are consequently associated with elevated risk, lending protocols offer lower leverage and concomitantly reduced risk exposure. The selection between perpetual futures and lending protocols in the operational framework of LVTs is contingent upon several factors, including: (i) the specific design and intended function of the token, (ii) the token's risk profile, (iii) the depth of liquidity provided by the underlying platform, and (iv) the investor's time horizon (short-term versus long-term). LVTs serve to abstract the complexities associated with maintaining leveraged positions, thereby simplifying position management for users by eliminating the need for continuous monitoring of margin requirements. The mechanism by which LVTs generate leverage for users relies on established financial markets, namely cryptocurrency derivatives and decentralized finance lending platforms. These markets offer efficient avenues for achieving desired leverage factors, typically up to 5× in LVTs. Leverage generation within derivatives markets is achieved through the utilization of instruments such as dated futures, perpetual contracts, or synthetic assets. Conversely, in DeFi lending markets, leverage is derived from the ability to borrow funds against collateral. Subsequent reinvestment of the borrowed capital amplifies exposure, thereby generating leverage for LVTs as reported in Fig. 3.4.

Fig. 3.4 A hierarchy of various types of crypto markets and instruments delineates the positions of the Futures and Lending markets (in blue)

3.4.3 Crypto Future Markets

A futures contract represents a standardized agreement to exchange a cryptocurrency at a predetermined price and future date. The cryptocurrency futures market facilitates the trading of these contracts, enabling participants to capitalize on anticipated price fluctuations. Futures contracts are classified as derivatives, often traded with significant leverage, thereby allowing traders to amplify their market exposure with reduced initial capital. This market supports both hedging strategies, designed to mitigate risk, and speculative activities, aimed at profiting from predicted price movements. Perpetual futures, a prevalent contract type within this market, allow traders to maintain leveraged positions indefinitely, without defined expiration dates. The principal risks associated with these derivative instruments include the accrual of funding fees and the potential for position liquidation.

3.5 Preventing Multiple Withdrawal Attack on ERC-20 Tokens

We provide an analysis of smart contracts with a specific focus on the ERC-20 token standard. Initially, we examine the Multiple Withdrawal Attack (MWA) vulnerability within ERC-20 tokens, which was identified in November 2016 and persists as an unresolved security concern lacking a definitive solution. Subsequently, we conduct a critical review of ten proposed mitigation strategies and present two novel proposals aimed at addressing this vulnerability. Implementation of either of these proposals is expected to substantially enhance the security posture of future ERC-20 smart contracts. Since the introduction of the ERC-20 standard in November 2015, a spectrum of security vulnerabilities has been identified. Notably, in November 2016, the MWA security issue was documented on GitHub (Vladimirov, 2016; Hale, 2017). This attack vector stems from the interaction of two methods within the ERC-20 standard, specifically those governing token approval and transfer. In adversarial environments, such as those susceptible to front-running (Eskandari et al., 2019), the utilization of these functions can result in the expenditure of a quantity of tokens exceeding the intended amount. Despite ongoing efforts, this vulnerability remains unresolved, with various mitigation proposals having been advanced. The ERC-20 application programming interface (API) defines the approve function, which grants a designated spender (e.g., user, wallet, or another smart contract) the authority to withdraw a specified allowance of tokens from the approver's token pool. Subsequent invocations of this function overwrite the existing allowance with the newly provided value. Conversely, the transferFrom function facilitates the actual transfer of tokens from the approver to a recipient specified by the spender, which may or may not be the spender themselves. The contract then updates the respective balances of the involved parties. A critical vulnerability arises from the temporal discrepancy between the confirmation of the approve and transferFrom functions. Specifically, the approve method's behavior of unconditionally replacing the current spender's allowance, irrespective of prior token transfers, creates an exploitable condition. This inherent functionality, dictated by the standard's specification, is immutable. Moreover, the dynamic state changes and logged events, while providing some information, are insufficient to definitively differentiate between potential execution traces. Consider the sequence of operations illustrated in Fig. 3.5, where the following sequence of events illustrates a vulnerability arising from the potential for front-running in token transfer approvals on the Ethereum blockchain:

1. Alice initiates an approval transaction, approve(Bob, N), authorizing Bob to transfer *N* tokens on her behalf.
2. Subsequently, Alice modifies Bob's approved transfer amount from *N* to *M* via a second approval transaction, approve(Bob, M).
3. Bob observes Alice's second transaction in the mempool, prior to its inclusion in a block, thus gaining awareness of the impending approval change.
4. Bob executes a front-running attack, specifically an asymmetric insertion attack as described (Eskandari et al., 2019) by submitting a transferFrom(Alice, Bob, N) transaction with an elevated gas price. This incentivizes a miner to prioritize Bob's transaction for inclusion in the next block, effectively transferring *N* tokens from Alice to Bob before her intended approval update.
5. Alice's second transaction, approve(Bob, M), is subsequently processed, altering Bob's approved transfer amount to *M*.
6. Consequently, Bob retains the ability to execute a further transferFrom transaction, transferring an additional *M* tokens from Alice's account.

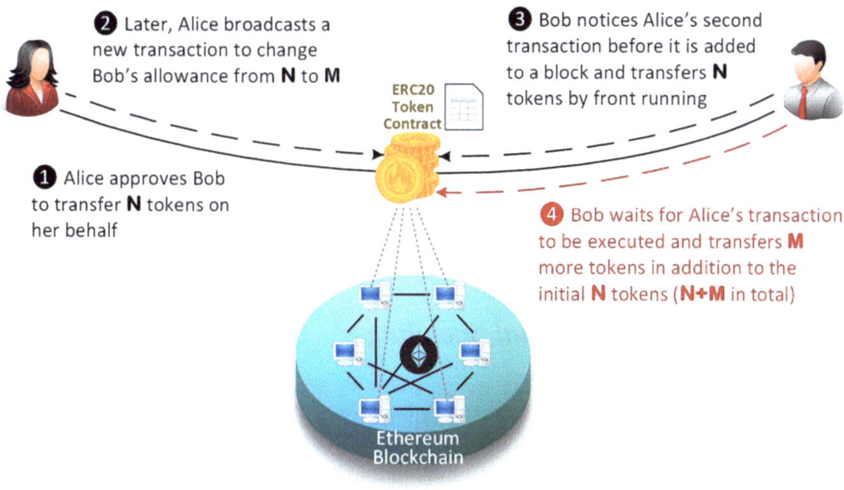

Fig. 3.5 MWA vulnerability process in ERC-20 tokens based on (Rahimian et al., 2019)

The process of modifying Bob's token allowance from N to M, as initiated by Alice, introduces a potential vulnerability whereby Bob could transfer N + M tokens from Alice's holdings. Assuming a robust implementation would preclude repeated withdrawals of Alice's tokens during the allowance transition, a viable solution must enforce a constraint limiting Bob's transfer capability to M tokens following the alteration from the initial N allowance. This mechanism would effectively mitigate the risk of unauthorized token transfers exceeding the intended M allocation.

3.5.1 Approval Process

Within the ERC-20 token standard, the allowance mechanism, implemented through the approve and transferFrom functions, facilitates delegated token expenditure. This mechanism enables a token owner to authorize a designated address, commonly a smart contract or third-party account, to transfer tokens from their balance. This indirect transfer paradigm, wherein authorization is granted prior to expenditure is employed in lieu of direct token transfers to contracts. This approach enhances security, flexibility, and usability within the ERC-20 framework.

3.5.2 Security: Prevents Loss of Funds

The direct transfer of ERC-20 tokens to smart contracts lacking explicit handling mechanisms for such transfers presents a significant risk of irreversible asset loss. Specifically, numerous smart contracts do not implement functionalities for the recovery of tokens erroneously transmitted via direct methods. For instance, consider a scenario where a user, Alice, intends to deposit tokens into a decentralized finance (DeFi) lending contract. If Alice utilizes the transfer method for direct token transmission, and the contract is not designed to process deposits via this mechanism, the tokens may become irretrievably locked or lost. In contrast, the employment of the approve and transferFrom functions facilitates a controlled token withdrawal by the contract, ensuring that tokens are only accessed when the contract is prepared to execute the intended transaction accurately.

3.5.3 Enables Conditional Spending

The approve followed by transferFrom pattern facilitates delegated token expenditure, enabling third-party contracts or users to utilize tokens on behalf of the owner under specified conditions. This mechanism is fundamental to numerous Decentralized finance applications. For instance, consider a scenario where Alice intends to deposit tokens into a *staking contract*, contingent upon the fulfillment of predefined criteria such as token price thresholds or gas fee levels. The staking contract can monitor these conditions and, upon their satisfaction, invoke the transferFrom function to transfer the tokens from Alice's balance. This approach empowers contracts to execute transfers only when necessary, thereby eliminating the requirement for repeated manual token transfers by the owner.

3.5.4 *Decentralized Authorization*

Instead of executing an immediate transfer of all token holdings, users possess the capability to define precise withdrawal allowances for designated third parties. This functionality offers substantial security enhancements by mitigating the risk associated with granting contracts unrestricted access to token reserves. Furthermore, it affords users granular control over token expenditures, enabling the establishment of specific limits for entities such as decentralized exchanges (DEXs), lending protocols, or escrow contracts. To illustrate, consider a scenario where Alice engages in token trading on a DEX. Instead of a blanket deposit of her entire token balance, which introduces potential security vulnerabilities, she can authorize the DEX to withdraw only the requisite quantity of tokens necessary for the intended trade.

3.5.5 *Gas Efficiency*

The utilization of the approve and transferFrom function combination within token transfer protocols can, in certain scenarios, yield significant gas savings relative to iterative manual transfers. For instance, in the context of yield farming contracts, a participant, such as Alice, can optimize transaction efficiency by granting the contract a pre-approved allowance. Rather than executing multiple individual transfer transactions, the contract autonomously retrieves the precise token quantity required in a singular transaction. This approach mitigates redundant transfer operations, thereby minimizing overall transaction costs and enhancing computational efficiency.

3.6 Conclusion

We presented an analysis of a critical vulnerability within the ERC-20 token standard, underscoring broader implications for blockchain development. The initial adoption of ERC-20, while fostering widespread tokenization and the ICO phenomenon (Fenu et al., 2018), inadvertently precipitated a landscape populated with numerous early, and often insecure, implementations. Consequently, the prevalence of exploitable ERC-20 tokens within decentralized exchanges necessitates urgent attention to the identified vulnerability—multiple withdrawal attack. While remediation of future ERC-20 deployments is achievable, the immutability of existing on-chain contracts presents a persistent challenge. Therefore, beyond the imperative of developing secure smart contracts, this chapter emphasizes the crucial role of rigorous external audits and the adoption of security-by-design principles across all smart contract implementations. These measures are essential to mitigate systemic risks and foster a more robust and secure blockchain ecosystem.

References

Block, T.. (2024). *Value locked by blockchain*. Retrieved October 16, 2024 from https://www.theblock.co/data/decentralized-finance/total-value-locked-tvl/value-locked-by-blockchain

Cheng, M., & Madhavan, A. (2009). The dynamics of leveraged and inverse exchange-traded funds. *Journal of Investment Management, 16*, 43.

Eskandari, S., Moosavi, S. & Clark, J. (2019). Sok: Transparent dishonesty: Front-running attacks on blockchain. In *International conference on financial cryptography and data security*.

Fabian Vogelsteller, V. B.. (2015). *Erc-20 token standard*. Retrieved October 16, 2024 from https://github.com/ethereum/ercs/blob/master/ERCS/erc-20.md

Fenu, G., Marchesi, L., Marchesi, M., & Tonelli, R. (2018). *The ico phenomenon and its relationships with ethereum smart contract environment* (pp. 26–32). IEEE.

Grand View Research. (2020). *Blockchain market size, share & trends analysis report by type (public, private, hybrid), by component, by application, by enterprise size, by end-use, by region, and segment forecasts, 2020–2027*. Retrieved October 16, 2024, from https://www.grandviewresearch.com/industry-analysis/blockchain-technology-market

Hale, T.. (2017). *Resolution on the EIP20 API Approve/Transfer from multiple withdrawal attack #738*. Retrieved December 5, 2018, from https://github.com/ethereum/EIPs/issues/738

Hayes, A.. (2023). *Volatility: Meaning in finance and how it works with stocks*. Retrieved May 19, 2023, from https://www.investopedia.com/terms/v/volatility.asp

Hill, J., & Foster, G. (2009). Understanding returns of leveraged and inverse funds. *Journal of Indexes, 12*, 40–58.

Labs, X.. (2020). *Advantages of blockchain in healthcare*. Retrieved October 16, 2024, from https://www.xcubelabs.com/blog/how-blockchain-will-benefit-the-healthcare-industry-in-2022-and-beyond/

Lettau, M., & Madhavan, A. (2018). Exchange-traded funds 101 for economists. *Journal of Economic Perspectives, 32*, 135–154.

Liebi, L. J. (2020). The effect of etfs on financial markets: A literature review. *Financial Markets and Portfolio Management, 34*, 165–178.

Luu, L., Chu, D.-H., Olickel, H., Saxena, P. & Hobor, A.. (2016). Making smart contracts smarter. *CCS'16.*

MarketsandMarkets. (2020, October 16). Blockchain market worth $39.7 billion by 2025. *PR Newswire.*

Rahimian, R., Eskandari, S., & Clark, J. (2019). *Resolving the multiple withdrawal attack on erc20 tokens* (pp. 320–329). IEEE.

Reportlinker. (2020). *Blockchain technology market worldwide is projected to grow by us $14.3 billion*. Retrieved October 16, 2024, from https://www.globenewswire.com/news-release/2020/05/20/2036593/0/en/Blockchain-Technology-market-worldwide-is-projected-to-grow-by-US-14-3-Billion.html

Securities, U., & Commission, E.. (2023). *Leveraged and inverse etfs: Specialized products with extra risks for buy-and-hold investors*. Retrieved May 2, 2023 from https://www.sec.gov/investor/pubs/leveragedetfs-alert

Siegel, D.. (2016). *Understanding the dao attack*. Retrieved October 16, 2024, from https://www.coindesk.com/understanding-dao-hack-journalists

Sristy, A.. (2021). *Blockchain in the food supply chain - What does the future look like?* https://tech.walmart.com/content/walmart-global-tech/en us/blog/post/blockchain-in-the-food-supply-chain.html

Stamford, C. (2019). *Gartner predicts 90% of current enterprise blockchain platform implementations will require replacement by 2021*. Retrieved October 1, 2024, from https://www.gartner.com/en/newsroom/press-releases/2019-07-03-gartner-predicts-90%2D%2Dof-current-enterprise-blockchain

Tracker, T.. (2020). *Erc-20 tokens*. Retrieved October 16, 2024, from https://etherscan.io/tokens

Vladimirov, M.. (2016). *Attack vector on ERC20 API (approve/transferFrom methods) and suggested improvements*. Retrieved December 18, 2018, from https://github.com/ethereum/EIPs/issues/20#issuecomment-263524729

Wided, K. (2019). On the properties of leveraged etfs. *Idea, 2*, 2.

Wood, G., et al. (2014). Ethereum: A secure decentralised generalised transaction ledger. *Ethereum project yellow paper, 151*, 1–32.

Amit Kumar Jaiswal A computer scientist and AI researcher specializes in quantum-inspired information retrieval, machine learning, and multimodal search. A recipient of Marie Skłodowska-Curie Fellow, he earned his Ph.D. from the University of Bedfordshire and has conducted AI-driven research at University College London, University of Surrey, and a visiting researcher at the University of Cambridge in AI for healthcare. He also worked at the University of Leeds with industry partners Credit Suisse and Finastra, developing synthetic data models for financial markets. He is currently a faculty chair of Jay Chaudhry Software innovation centre at IIT (BHU) Varanasi.

Chapter 4
Sybil Detection in Web3 Airdrops: Challenges and Solutions

Yihan Sun, Katherine Webb, Mohamed Ezeldin, Valerii Anufriev, Cedric Lion, and Ming Ruan

4.1 Introduction to Web3 Airdrop

An airdrop is a mechanism for distributing tokens to users. This can be done by airdropping tokens directly into a user's wallet or through a claim mechanism. Airdrops serve as a key growth strategy in Web3, helping projects drive adoption, decentralize governance, and boost liquidity without relying on traditional fundraising or marketing (Arbitrum Foundation, 2023). The top 50 airdrops between 2020 and 2023 distributed $26.6B worth of token (Boey, 2024). Airdrops foster engagement, reward loyalty, and amplify network effects by targeting specific groups, like early adopters, active traders, or ecosystem participants. Airdrops also play a crucial role in decentralizing governance, as seen with ApeCoin (APE) and rewarding early supporters through retroactive distributions, such as Uniswap (UNI). Additionally, as demonstrated by HyperLiquid (HLP), they can accelerate product-market fit or boost liquidity ahead of exchange listings, as seen with Aptos (APT). When strategically executed, airdrops align incentives, foster engagement, and drive long-term adoption.

Animoca Brands: A Web3 leader that leverages tokenization and blockchain to deliver digital property rights. Animoca Brands' business includes: (1) operating Web3 businesses to advance blockchain adoption; (2) providing digital asset advisory services including tokenomics advisory, liquidity provisioning, and institutional research to help external Web3 projects grow; and (3) investment management, with a portfolio of investments in over 540 companies including Yuga Labs, OpenSea, and Polygon.

Y. Sun · M. Ruan (✉)
Animoca Brands Limited, Hong Kong, China
e-mail: mingr@animocabrands.com

K. Webb · M. Ezeldin · V. Anufriev · C. Lion
Animoca Brands Limited, London, UK

Y. Xiong (ed.), *Blockchain Analytics for Practitioners*, Business Analytics in Practice, https://doi.org/10.1007/978-3-032-06046-4_4

Despite the benefits, airdrops face a significant challenge from "Sybil" attacks—where a single entity creates multiple wallets, known as "Sybil wallets," to unfairly claim excessive token allocations (Arbitrum DAO, 2025; Platt and McBurney, 2023). The term "Sybil attack" originates from a 1973 book titled *Sybil*, which depicted a character with multiple personalities. This practice, often called airdrop farming, artificially inflates the user base and centralizes token supply under the control of a few actors, undermining fairness and project sustainability (Imperva, 2025). Additionally, Sybil farmers can create sudden selling pressure by offloading large volumes of tokens at once, disrupting token economics. (Messias et al., 2023).

4.2 Methods in Addressing Sybil Problem

Detecting Sybil wallets in cryptocurrency networks requires a combination of analytical and non-analytical approaches (Beosin, 2023). Analytical methods provide scalable, data-driven solutions for identifying suspicious patterns by analyzing wallet transaction histories to detect unnatural behaviors (Yu et al., 2006). These methods are computationally intensive and often need to be prepared in advance to be effectively applied before an airdrop. Non-analytical approaches, such as identity verification through KYC compliance, proof-of-humanity protocols, and social credentials, offer additional layers of validation (Matsuoka and Lazzarin, 2024). Combining both analytical and non-analytical techniques enhances Sybil resistance, ensuring a more effective and fair token distribution.

4.2.1 Analytical Approach

Analytical approaches leverage machine learning models and data-driven techniques to detect Sybil accounts. This paper explores two commonly used methods: network analysis and clustering analysis. Network analysis examines transaction networks between wallets to identify closely linked wallet communities that may indicate Sybil wallets (Allium, 2024). Clustering analysis, on the other hand, focuses on behavioral patterns, detecting wallets that exhibit suspicious, Sybil-like actions (Trusta Labs, 2023).

4.2.2 Network Analysis

The Louvain method has emerged as the most practical and widely used choice for detecting communities within transaction networks, particularly in the context of cryptocurrency networks (Wormhole, 2024). The Louvain method strikes the perfect balance—it is computationally efficient, scalable for large networks, and produces reliable, high-quality results. Other methods, such as spectral methods, can provide accurate results for smaller datasets but struggle with the scale of large transaction networks. On the other hand, simpler methods, such as label propagation, are faster but lack consistency and reliability, making their results harder to trust.

The Louvain method is a network analysis algorithm designed to identify meaningful structures within large, interconnected systems. This method begins by assigning each node to its own community and iteratively merges nodes and communities to maximize modularity. This hierarchical approach allows the Louvain method to identify densely connected groups of nodes (communities) within a network while being computationally efficient and scalable, even for very large datasets.

In the context of cryptocurrency networks, the Louvain method analyzes transaction data as a network of nodes (wallets) and edges (transactions), and then groups wallets into communities based on their interaction patterns. Suspiciously dense or isolated communities, with nodes that disproportionately interact among themselves rather than with the broader network, may indicate Sybil activity.

The Louvain method is designed to maximize modularity, a measure of the quality of a partition of the network into communities. Modularity evaluates how well nodes are grouped, comparing the actual connections within a community to the expected number of connections if edges were randomly distributed (Blondel et al., 2008). To calculate modularity, the following variables are used: A_{ij} is the actual edges (transactions) between nodes i and j. k_i and k_j are the sum of edges (i.e., transactions) connected to nodes i and j, respectively. m is the total number of edges (transactions) in the network. γ, also called resolution, is a hyperparameter to adjust cluster sizes. c_i and c_j are the clusters that nodes i and j belong to. The delta function $\delta(c_i, c_j)$ here is defined as: 1 if nodes i and j are in the same cluster, and 0 if not. The formula for modularity is:

$$\text{Modularity} = \frac{1}{2m} \Sigma_{i,j} \left(A_{ij} - \gamma \frac{k_i k_j}{2m} \right) \times \delta\left(c_i, c_j\right)$$

In this formula, A_{ij} counts the direct connections between nodes within the same cluster. $\frac{k_i k_j}{2m}$ denotes the expected number of edges between nodes i and j if edges were randomly distributed. The hyperparameter γ modifies the impact of expected random connections. Larger γ value encourages small clusters by increasing the impact of the expected random connections, and vice versa. $\delta(c_i, c_j)$ ensures that only pairs of nodes within the same cluster contribute to the modularity score. Collectively, the above elements measure how densely connected nodes are within a cluster compared to random connections (Blondel et al., 2008).

The Louvain method works iteratively in two steps:

1. *Local Optimization*: Initially, each node is assigned to its own community. The algorithm then evaluates the modularity gain for moving a node into one of its neighboring communities. The node is moved to a neighboring community if it increases modularity. This step repeats for all nodes until no further modularity improvement is possible.
2. *Network Compression*: Once no further modularity improvement can be achieved through single node assignment, the algorithm moves on to aggregate the network. Each community from the previous step is treated as a single "supernode" in a new, smaller network. The weight of the edges between supernodes is the sum of the cross-community edges. This compression step simplifies the network while preserving its structure for further optimization. With the new aggregated network, the Louvain method repeats the optimization and compression until the modularity score converges and no further improvements can be achieved.

The optimized modularity value ensures that the detected clusters maximize internal connections while minimizing external ones, capturing the natural structure of the network (Fig. 4.1).

To better understand the algorithm, let us walk through a step-by-step example with dummy transactions and illustrate its iterations visually: Imagine a network of six nodes (A, B, C, D, E, F) connected by weighted edges that represent the number of transactions between nodes. The connections are as follows: A $\leftrightarrow$ B (weight: 3), A $\leftrightarrow$ C (weight: 2), B $\leftrightarrow$ C (weight: 4), B $\leftrightarrow$ D (weight: 1), C $\leftrightarrow$ E (weight: 5), and D $\leftrightarrow$ F (weight: 2). Initially, each node starts as its own community. At this stage, the communities are {A}, {B}, {C}, {D}, {E}, and {F}.

In the Local Optimization step, the algorithm evaluates the modularity gain of moving each node into the community of one of its neighbors. For example, consider node A. The algorithm calculates the modularity gain if A is moved to B's community or C's community. If moving A to B's community results in the highest modularity gain, the algorithm moves A. This process is repeated for all nodes. After one iteration of local optimization, some nodes join larger communities where modularity is higher. For instance, nodes A, B, and C may form a single community, while nodes D, E, and F remain separate. At this point, the communities are {A, B, C}, {D}, {E}, and {F}.

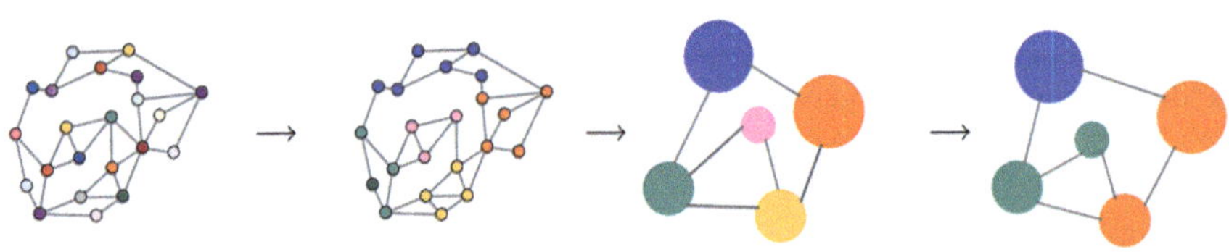

Fig. 4.1 Illustration of the Louvain algorithm's stages (Adapted from https://www.researchgate.net/figure/The-two-stages-of-the-Louvain-algorithm-a-In-the-first-the-algorithm-passes-through_fig1_362977252)

Once no further modularity improvement is possible by moving individual nodes, the algorithm proceeds to the Network Compression step. In this step, the current communities are treated as single "supernodes," and the network is aggregated to form a smaller network. The weight of the edge between two supernodes is calculated as the sum of the weights of the edges between the nodes in the respective communities. For example, if the community {A, B, C} is connected to node E through an edge C $\leftrightarrow$ E with a weight of 5, the weight of the edge between the supernode {A, B, C} and the supernode {E} in the compressed network is 5. The Louvain method then repeats the Local Optimization and Network Compression steps on this smaller network.

This iterative process continues until modularity converges, meaning no further improvements can be made. In our example, after a few iterations, the algorithm may detect two final communities: {A, B, C, E} and {D, F}. These communities represent clusters where the connections within each cluster are denser than those between clusters.

4.2.3 Clustering Analysis

Clustering analysis groups wallets based on behavioral similarities. In cryptocurrency systems, clustering methods are used to identify suspicious groups of accounts that exhibit coordinated activity, which is a hallmark of Sybil attacks. Among the available options, OPTICS (Ordering Points to Identify the Clustering Structure) stands out as a powerful and effective approach for Sybil detection compared to other clustering methods.

Many clustering methods such as k-means, DBSCAN (Density-Based Spatial Clustering of Applications with Noise), and hierarchical clustering are also available. While these methods are widely used in various applications, they often fall short when applied to the unique challenges of cryptocurrency networks. K-means, for example, requires the number of clusters to be predefined, which is impractical in Sybil detection since the number of suspicious groups is unknown. Additionally, k-means struggles to handle irregular or complex data distributions, which are common in cryptocurrency transaction patterns.

DBSCAN, another popular method, performs better in detecting clusters of uniform densities and can identify outliers. For example, DBSCAN is well-suited for detecting clusters in geographical data, where clusters tend to have similar densities (e.g., identifying groups of cities or regions). However, it can fail when the data contains clusters with significantly different densities.

Hierarchical clustering, on the other hand, provides a detailed tree-like structure of clusters, which can be useful for analyzing relationships between clusters. But it is computationally expensive and unsuitable for large-scale datasets like cryptocurrency transaction networks, where millions of wallets and transactions must be analyzed.

OPTICS addresses many of these limitations by analyzing the density of "points" to identify clusters (Ankerst et al., 1999). In the context of cryptocurrency, wallets can be thought of as points, and their relationships, such as transaction volumes or frequencies, help determine the density around each wallet. Unlike the three clustering methods mentioned above, OPTICS does not require the number of clusters to be predefined. It is capable of handling clusters with varying densities and is relatively efficient in terms of computational cost. Table 4.1 summarizes the trade-offs between DBSCAN, k-means, hierarchical clustering, and OPTICS:

OPTICS starts by defining actual distance between points and computes the core distance and reachability distance for each point. These distances help determine which points belong to dense regions and how tightly connected they are.

The actual distance is subject to definition of each analysis and is often defined in Euclidean distance form based on numerical features of points such as transaction frequency of a wallet. The core distance is the smallest distance at which a point has enough neighbors (at least *MinPts* neighbors) within a specified radius (ε) to be considered part of a dense region. Points that meet this condition are known as core points. The reachability distance, on the other hand, is defined for each point as the greater of its core distance and the distance to another point. This ensures that a point is only considered reachable if it is part of a dense region or connected to one. The core distance and reachability distance are crucial for determining clusters, where *MinPts* is the minimum number of points required to form a cluster (Fig. 4.2).

We may better understand the two distances from the illustration above. Here, point A is being analyzed with $MinPts = 5$. The core distance of A is the distance to the fifth closest point within its neighborhood (the radius is shown as the circle around A). In this case, the core distance of A is 0.4489609, as the fifth nearest

Table 4.1 Comparison of clustering methods for Sybil detection

Clustering method	Advantages	Disadvantages	Suitability for Sybil detection
k-means	Simple and fast for well-separated, spherical clusters.	Requires predefined number of clusters; struggles with irregular or complex distributions.	Low—Sybil clusters are often irregular and not predefined.
DBSCAN	Can detect arbitrarily shaped clusters and outliers.	Struggles with clusters of varying densities.	Medium—Works well for uniform densities but fails with diverse Sybil behaviors.
Hierarchical clustering	Provides a detailed hierarchy of clusters; does not require predefined cluster numbers.	Computationally expensive for large datasets; not scalable to millions of wallets.	Medium—Computational cost makes it not ideal for Sybil detection.
OPTICS	Handles varying densities; does not require predefined cluster numbers.	Computationally more expensive than DBSCAN but scalable for large datasets.	High—Ideal for detecting diverse Sybil attack patterns.

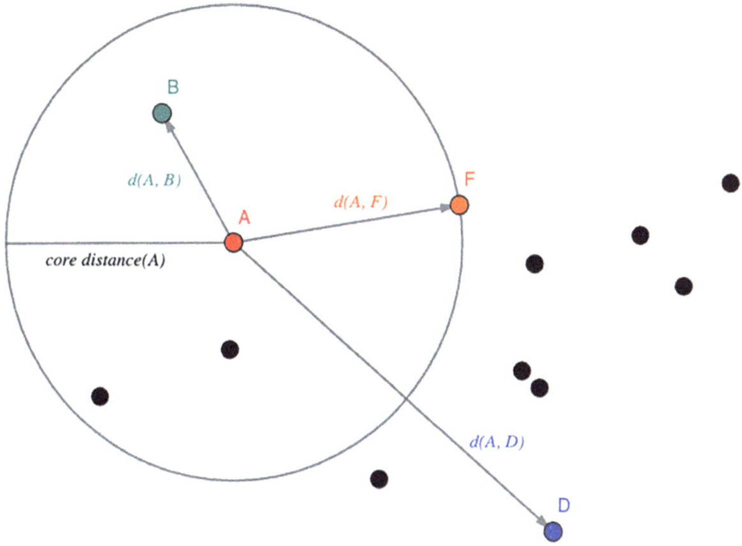

$minPoints = 5$

$$\left.\begin{array}{l} d(A, F) = 0.4489609 = core\ distance(A) \\ d(A, B) = 0.3452897 < core\ distance(A) \\ d(A, D) = 0.9740773 > core\ distance(A) \end{array}\right\} \Rightarrow \begin{array}{l} reachability\ distance(B, A) = core\ distance(A) = 0.4489609 \\ reachability\ distance(F, A) = core\ distance(A) = 0.4489609 \\ reachability\ distance(D, A) = d(A, D) = 0.9740773 \end{array}$$

Fig. 4.2 Illustration of core distance and reachability distance in OPTICS clustering (Adopted from https://www.atlantbh.com/clustering-algorithms-dbscan-vs-optics)

neighbor lies at this distance. For the reachability distance, we compare the core distance of A with the actual distance to other points. For example, the reachability distance to B is equal to the core distance of A since the distance between A and B (0.3452897) is smaller than the core distance. Similarly, the reachability distance to F is also equal to the core distance of A. However, for point D, which lies outside the core distance of A, the reachability distance is simply the actual distance between A and D (0.9740773). This demonstrates how both distances help define dense regions and connections between points.

After deciding core and reachability distances for each point, the algorithm processes the points in a specific order to reflect how clusters grow based on density connectivity. This order is determined by expanding clusters starting from one point and systematically exploring their neighbors, prioritizing densely connected regions before moving to sparser areas.

More specifically, the algorithm begins by selecting an arbitrary point in the dataset and calculating its core distance. It then examines all neighbors within radius ε, computing their reachability distances relative to the starting point. Points with lower reachability distances are processed first, as they are closer and part of denser regions, while points in sparser areas or noise are processed later.

After finishing the processing of all points within the radius ε (i.e., the current neighborhood), the algorithm moves on to the next unvisited point in the dataset. If this new point is not density-reachable from any previously processed point, its reachability distance is set to a higher value, signifying that it is isolated or part of a sparse region. The algorithm then computes the core distance for the new point and begins a new cluster expansion if it qualifies as having at least *MinPts* neighbors within ε. If not, the point is treated as noise.

This step-by-step exploration ensures that points are ordered based on their reachability distances as the algorithm expands density-connected clusters. The resulting ordered sequence of points is used to construct the reachability plot. On the plot, the x-axis represents the order in which points are processed, while the y-axis shows the reachability distance of each point as it is visited. Dense clusters appear as valleys in the plot, where points are tightly packed and have low reachability distances, while sparse regions or noise appear as peaks, where reachability distances are higher due to the lack of dense connectivity (Fig. 4.3).

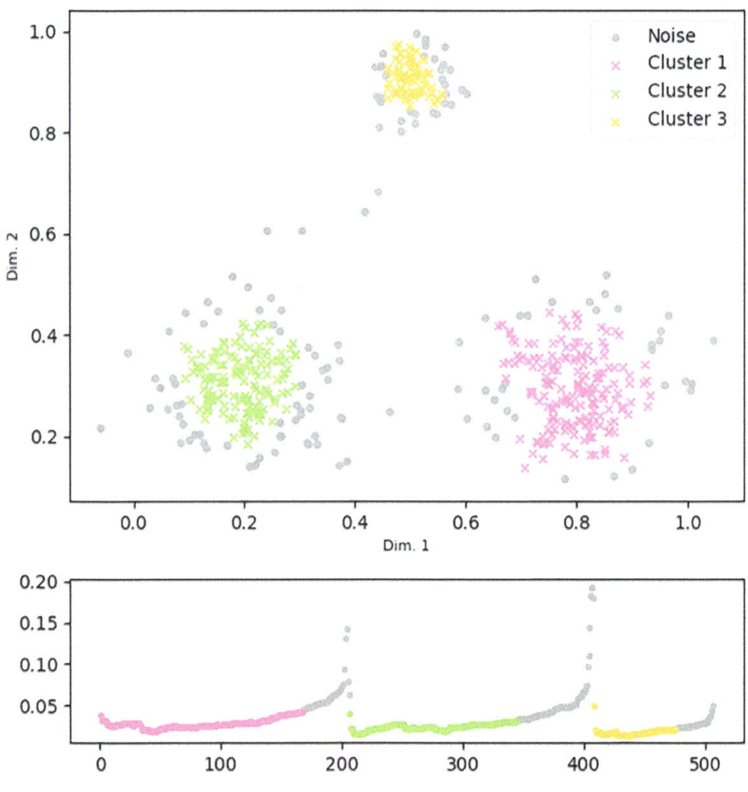

Fig. 4.3 Visualization of a 2D dataset and its corresponding reachability plot (Adopted from https://www.researchgate.net/figure/Reachability-plot-for-a-sample-2D-data-set-visualization-with-ELKI-Schubert-Zimek_fig5_336892821)

4.2.4 Non-Analytical Approach

Non-analytical methods, such as self or community reporting, referencing known Sybil wallet lists, and using proof-of-humanity or identity verification systems, provide alternative ways to enhance projects' ability to detect Sybil wallets (Beosin, 2023; Matsuoka and Lazzarin, 2024; Passport XYZ, 2024). Unlike purely algorithmic or data-driven approaches, these methods rely on leveraging external information that goes beyond wallet transactions and blockchain activity. They can be particularly useful in incorporating human judgment or external verification mechanisms into the detection process (Gitcoin, 2021; Imperva, 2025).

Here are few example methods.

1. Community Reporting:
   This method involves crowdsourcing information from a project's user base. Users or participants report suspicious wallets, often incentivized by rewards or recognition. This approach can be effective in identifying Sybil wallets that evade automated detection but requires active participation and consistent moderation to ensure accuracy and prevent abuse.
2. Proof-of-Humanity Systems:
   Proof-of-humanity protocols require users to verify their identity through methods such as facial recognition, document verification, or social proof (e.g., endorsements from other verified users). These systems, such as Proof of Humanity or BrightID, are designed to establish a user's uniqueness, reducing the risk of Sybil attacks. However, they raise concerns about privacy, accessibility, and scalability, especially in decentralized environments (Arbitrum DAO, 2025).
3. Referencing Known Sybil Wallet Lists:
   By maintaining and consulting lists of wallets previously identified as Sybil actors, projects can cross-check new participants during an airdrop campaign. While this is a practical approach, the accuracy and timeliness of these lists are critical. Outdated or incomplete lists may lead to false positives or negatives.
4. Self-Reporting:
   Users may voluntarily provide information, such as their social media profiles or proof of participation in other communities, to verify their identity. While this approach is low-cost, it relies heavily on trust and may be prone to manipulation.

Non-analytical approaches allow for the incorporation of human judgment, which can capture nuances and context that purely analytical methods might overlook. These methods are also highly flexible, enabling projects to tailor their approach to specific needs. On the other hand, these approaches also present limitations. Community reporting requires sustained engagement, proper incentives, and consistent moderation to remain reliable, which can be resource-intensive. Proof-of-humanity and identity verification methods may introduce friction in the user experience, potentially deterring users from participating and raising privacy concerns. Furthermore, implementing and maintaining these systems can increase operational costs, and scalability remains a significant issue for projects with large or rapidly growing user bases.

4.3 An Integrated Analytical Approach in Sybil Detection

The combination of network analysis and clustering techniques is particularly effective in identifying tightly connected Sybil groups and providing insights into their structure and behavior. Network analysis pinpoints communities of wallets that are likely collaborating based on their transaction patterns, while cluster analysis classifies the roles within these groups (e.g., master wallets versus minion wallets). This layered approach enhances detection accuracy and enables projects to tailor their responses to specific wallet behaviors.

In our practice, the Louvain method is used for community detection to identify cohesive groups within the network, and OPTICS is used for cluster analysis to classify roles within these groups. In this section, we will discuss details in applying these two methods and model calibrations.

4.3.1 Step 1: Louvain Network Analysis

When applying the Louvain method in practice, steps are taken in order to achieve useful results. Here are a few examples:

Exclude non-user wallet address: Blockchain addresses include not only individual user wallets, but also smart contracts and operational wallets owned by institutions such as crypto exchanges. These wallets or addresses often have high transaction frequencies with user wallets but are not relevant to Sybil behaviors. Removing these addresses ensures that the analysis focuses on individual users and avoids false positives caused by high-activity nodes. Similarly, care should be taken to account for noise or irregularities in the network, such as one-off transactions or inactive accounts, which can skew the results.

Define the edge function: The edge function defines the strength of connections, also referred to as "weights," between wallets in the network. These weights play a critical role in the cluster detection process, as stronger connections are more likely to group wallets into the same cluster. Properly defining the edge function is essential for the Louvain method to effectively identify meaningful clusters, especially in the context of Sybil detection. Common approaches for defining edge weights include using the number of transactions between wallets or the total value of transactions exchanged between them.

Determine resolution: The resolution parameter (γ) plays a critical role in determining the size and number of clusters in community detection. A higher resolution value tends to produce smaller, more granular clusters, potentially leading to over-segmentation, while a lower resolution value results in larger, coarser clusters, which may cause under-segmentation. Striking the right balance is crucial for obtaining meaningful and interpretable results. There are multiple methods developed for deciding the value of the resolution parameter. One common approach is to use domain-specific knowledge to guide the choice of resolution, ensuring that the detected clusters align with real-world expectations or known patterns in the data. Alternatively, heuristic methods, such as comparing modularity across different resolution values, can help identify an optimal range by selecting the value that maximizes modularity or other clustering quality metrics. Sensitivity analysis is another technique, where the resolution parameter is varied systematically, and the stability of the resulting clusters is evaluated to find a value that produces consistent and reliable groupings.

4.3.2 Step 2: Clustering Analysis with OPTICS

After using network analysis to identify communities, i.e., potential groups of Sybils, clustering analysis can be deployed to refine the result. The main goal of the clustering analysis is to distinguish Sybil wallets from normal wallets within each community based on wallet behavioral patterns. The underlying assumption is that Sybil wallets within a group tend to exhibit similar behaviors, while normal wallets (or outliers within a community) deviate from this homogeneous behavior (Allium, 2024). Here are a few considerations in properly deploying the analysis:

Define the actual distance function: The calculation of both core distance and reachability distance relies on the actual distance, making it essential to define this function carefully. Typically, the actual distance is calculated using numerical behavioral features, such as transaction frequency, transaction volume, and timing patterns.

Exclude the core of the cluster: Before performing clustering, it is important to consider excluding the "core" of the cluster—the most densely connected node in the community—from the OPTICS analysis. The core often represents the controlling entity of the Sybil community and may exhibit behavior distinct from the surrounding minions. For instance, the core might engage in a more diverse range of transactions or interact with external wallets, making its behavior less uniform compared to its minions. Excluding the core helps preserve the assumption of behavioral uniformity among the minions, resulting in more accurate and meaningful clustering outcomes.

Tune hyper-parameters: Proper tuning of MinPts and ε is critical for achieving meaningful clustering results with OPTICS. The selection of MinPts often depends on domain knowledge, such as the expected minimum number of similar wallets in a dense region. Through iterative experimentation, analysis, and domain knowledge, these parameters can be fine-tuned to produce meaningful clustering results.

Refine clusters: Once the OPTICS algorithm has been applied, the resulting clusters can be refined for better classification. Wallets identified as outliers—those that do not belong to any dense cluster—can be classified as normal wallets, as their behaviors do not align with the homogeneity typically exhibited by Sybil wallets.

The remaining dense clusters, characterized by highly similar behavioral patterns among their members, are then classified as Sybil groups. This refinement ensures a clear distinction between normal wallets and Sybil entities, improving the accuracy of the detection process.

4.3.3 Step 3: Model Calibration

Reliable data is essential for calibrating the analytical model and accurately identifying Sybil wallets. Due to the decentralized nature of the crypto space, there is no central authority to provide certified Sybil lists. Alternatively, one may use proprietary airdrop data or third-party marketing campaign data for model calibration.

In our cases, proprietary data can be obtained from past Animoca Brands campaigns that involved airdrops to wallets. Some of these wallets displayed Sybil-like behaviors after receiving airdrops, such as consolidating received tokens into a single address. To construct our training set, we used pre-airdrop wallet transactions as input data and post-airdrop wallet behavior as the "ground truth." It is important to note that this approach may include false negatives—wallets that do not immediately exhibit Sybil-like behavior after the airdrop but may still be Sybil wallets that have not yet taken action.

One well-known third-party data example is LayerZero's Sybil and airdrop datasets. LayerZero, an omnichain interoperability protocol that enables seamless communication and asset transfers across blockchains, launched an anti-Sybil campaign in May 2024 before conducting its airdrop. This campaign resulted in the release of a Sybil wallet list, which we used for model evaluation. However, the third-party data also has limitations. The accuracy of the Sybil list is not guaranteed, and there is no information about which blockchain transaction data was used in Sybil detection.

By combining proprietary and third-party campaign data, the model can be properly calibrated and applied to future campaign design and on-chain user labeling.

4.4 Other Considerations in Airdrop Design

Airdrop campaigns vary in scope, complexity, and strategic intent, but they share a core objective: driving meaningful user engagement and fostering strong network effects. To design an effective airdrop, the project must clearly define its goals, tailor distribution models to align with user behavior and ensure fair allocations. Identifying Sybil wallets is crucial in this process, as it allows the project to eliminate or penalize exploitative actors, ensuring that legitimate users are rewarded fairly.

Beyond Sybil detection, several key factors should be considered to maximize the impact and sustainability of an airdrop:

4.4.1 Define Clear Objectives

Determine whether the airdrop aims to attract new users or reward existing ones. For instance, Uniswap rewarded early adopters by distributing 400 UNI tokens to users who had previously interacted with the platform, recognizing their prior engagement. Blast Designed its airdrop to encourage users to bridge assets to their Layer 2 network. Users earn Blast Points based on the volume of assets bridged and can accumulate additional points through activities on the platform. Projects often distribute tokens to multiple user cohorts, for instance, holders of other tokens or NFTs, to expand reach and foster cross-community engagement. One example was the $PENGU token by Pudgy Penguins, which other token or NFT holder communities might also be eligible to participate $PENGU claim.

4.4.2 Crafting a Tailored Reward Framework

Effective airdrop design demands a nuanced approach to user segmentation and incentive calibration. This begins by categorizing ecosystem participants such as traders, governance contributors, or NFT holders and weighting their actions based on effort, cost, and investment. For instance, staking (which requires capital lockup and long-term commitment) might merit greater rewards than low-effort tasks like social media shares. Blanket rewards should be avoided to prevent diluting token value or misaligning incentives between casual users and high-impact contributors. The eligibility for an airdrop can be defined based on transaction history, governance participation, or the holding of specific assets to encourage "mission-aligned" recipients. For example, dYdX diversified its criteria by incorporating user engagement metrics, such as staking, governance voting, and bridging. Projects must balance incentives to achieve the desired outcomes for user acquisition and retention.

A robust reward structure hinges on two pillars:

1. Identifying Eligible Participants: Define clear criteria tied to on-chain activity (e.g., transaction volume, governance votes) or asset ownership (e.g., holding specific NFTs).
2. Balancing Proportionality: Reward allocations should reflect each group's time, resources, and risks.

4.4.3 Mitigate Post-Airdrop Selling Pressure

Airdrop distributions often trigger immediate sell pressure, which can destabilize token value. Implementing economic and time-based incentives helps mitigate this risk. One effective approach is a "Claim Now - Claim Later" function where users who delay their claim receive additional rewards. Open Campus employed this method for their EDU airdrop to Genesis NFT holders. NFT holders had the option to either: claim all now, claim 50% now and 50% later, or claim all later with an additional bonus for the later claim.

Multi-staged airdrops offer another way to reduce sell pressure while maintaining user engagement. Instead of distributing all tokens at once, projects can structure airdrops in phases, adjusting eligibility criteria and reward structures based on community behavior. Optimism, for example, rolled out multiple airdrop rounds, refining its distribution strategy over time to encourage long-term participation.

Beyond structured claims, creating real utility for airdropped tokens is key to preventing mass liquidation. Providing staking options, governance rights, or in-app use cases encourages recipients to hold and engage rather than immediately offload their tokens. In 2024, MOCA airdropped tokens to NFT and MocaID holders, giving them the ability to stake both assets to earn additional staking power, reinforcing token demand and long-term value retention (Mocaverse, 2024).

By designing claim mechanics, reward schedules, and token utilities with longevity in mind, projects can prevent airdrops from becoming short-term exit opportunities and instead use them as tools for sustainable ecosystem growth.

4.5 Airdrop Case Examples

4.5.1 LayerZero: Cross-Chain Interoperability Protocol

LayerZero, a cross-chain interoperability protocol supporting over 100 chains and engaging with over six million wallets, implemented a robust anti-Sybil strategy before its June 2024 airdrop. The project employed on-chain analysis to cluster wallets associated with large-scale Sybil farming activities, identifying those minting "valueless" NFTs solely for cross-chain movement and those conducting minimal-value transactions ($0.01) to simulate authentic activity. Additionally, wallets that utilized popular Sybil farming applications like Merkly, L2Pass, and L2Marathon were excluded. LayerZero also introduced a self-reporting mechanism to enhance the filtering process, offering Sybil actors 15% of their intended allocation if they disclosed their activities within 14 days, leading to 100,000 wallets self-reporting. The project adopted a two-phase approach: first, it disqualified Sybil wallets identified internally that had not self-reported; second, it opened a bounty program, rewarding individuals with 10% of the allocation destined for a Sybil wallet for successful reports.

The impact of these measures was significant: daily messages on the protocol plummeted from 300,000 to 50,000 after the Sybil detection announcement. Despite this decline, LayerZero sustained its leading position in the cross-chain messaging sector, maintaining approximately 80% market share alongside competitors like Wormhole, Axelar, and CCIP.

4.5.2 Uniswap: Decentralized Crypto Exchange

Uniswap, a DEX on Ethereum, conducted its notable $UNI airdrop on September 17th, 2020 (Uniswap Labs, 2020). This airdrop distributed tokens to over 250,000 addresses that had interacted with the protocol before September first, 2020. The eligibility criteria included historical users of Uniswap Versions 1 and 2, liquidity providers, and $SOCKS redeemers. A critical anti-Sybil measure employed by Uniswap was the retroactive nature of the airdrop. By not announcing the airdrop beforehand, Uniswap significantly reduced incentives for Sybil farming. This approach ensured that the airdrop was primarily claimed by genuine users who had organically interacted with the protocol.

However, post-airdrop analyses indicated that most recipients promptly sold their tokens. Dune Analytics report (Nov 2022) revealed that only 6.7% of wallets still held $UNI, with a mere 2% retaining the original allocation and just 0.6% increasing their $UNI holdings over time. The primary objectives of the airdrop were to decentralize governance and reward early adopters. Additionally, Uniswap aimed to counteract "vampire attacks" from competitors like SushiSwap, which attempted to siphon Uniswap's liquidity by offering rival incentives. By rewarding its loyal user base, Uniswap secured its position as Ethereum's leading, with $UNI becoming a top DeFi governance token.

4.5.3 Optimism: Ethereum Layer-2 Scaling Solution

Optimism, a prominent layer-2 scaling solution for Ethereum, leveraging optimistic rollup technology, executed a multi-staged airdrop beginning on May 31st, 2022. Optimism adopted a rigorous eligibility framework to mitigate Sybil attacks. This approach successfully excluded low-activity and newly created addresses, common vectors for Sybil exploitation. Additionally, Optimism implemented a tiered airdrop structure, segmenting eligible wallets based on behavioral patterns. This tiered approach rewarded consistent and recurrent usage over one-time interactions, fostering a more engaged and mission-aligned user base.

The strict eligibility criteria proved effective, filtering out approximately 17,000 Sybil addresses and preserving nearly 14 million $OP tokens, valued at around $19.6 million during the first airdrop stage. Although the strategy significantly reduced fraudulent claims, it had potential drawbacks. The stringent measures inadvertently excluded legitimate participants, possibly limiting the overall diversity and growth of the community. Furthermore, some sophisticated farmers bypassed these controls by conducting low-value, high-frequency transactions that mimicked authentic user behavior. Nevertheless, Optimism's tiered distribution model remains a noteworthy example of how thoughtfully designed eligibility requirements can enhance the integrity of token distributions while promoting sustained user engagement.

4.5.4 *Jupiter: Solana-Based Liquidity Aggregator*

Jupiter, a Solana-based liquidity aggregator, initiated a multi-stage airdrop of its $JUP token, with the first phase in January 2024 and the second in January 2025. To combat Sybil attacks, Jupiter required users to create profiles linked to unique email addresses and wallet connections, ensuring one profile per email. They also implemented measures to exclude circular transactions below $5 and discounted stablecoin-to-stablecoin and SOL-to-SOL swaps, focusing only on tokens with reliable price data. These strategies aimed to deter malicious actors employing multiple wallets or wash trading tactics. Despite these efforts, some users managed to link various wallets to a single profile, and there were concerns about privacy due to the email linkage. In cases where wallets were mistakenly labeled as Sybil, users were allowed to appeal the decision after January 27th, 2025, during the 3-month claim period. As of the time of writing, Dune Analytics data show over 46% of the second airdrop has been claimed, with 14.1% of these wallets retaining their $JUP tokens and 87.2% of those having acquired additional $JUP tokens.

4.6 Conclusion

Token airdrops are a unique growth mechanism in Web3 ecosystems that can foster user engagement, but they are also vulnerable to Sybil attacks, where multiple wallets are created to exploit token allocations (Messias et al., 2023). These attacks threaten the fairness, decentralization, and economic viability of airdrop campaigns. A multi-faceted approach is required to address the Sybil problem, combining analytical techniques such as the Louvain method for network analysis and OPTICS for clustering with non-analytical measures like proof-of-humanity protocols and self-reporting incentives.

There are also emerging trends that could further influence approaches to Sybil detection. On one hand, crypto farmers, those controlling Sybil wallets, are becoming more adept at using their wallets to evade detection algorithms. On the other hand, the rapid advancement of neural network algorithms and AI offers opportunities to develop more sophisticated pattern recognition techniques for identifying Sybil activity.

In addition, successful airdrop design requires considerations beyond Sybil detection, including the trade-offs between detection rigor and user inclusivity and the limitations of calibration data in a decentralized context. Future airdrop designs must prioritize adaptive frameworks that integrate advanced analytics with user-centric considerations, ensuring that token distributions resist manipulation and cultivate genuine, long-term participation.

References

Allium. (2024, May 1). Drift partners with Allium for Sybil analysis and detection. Available at: https://www.allium.so/post/drift-partners-with-allium-for-sybil-analysis-and-detection. Accessed 25 February 2025.

Ankerst, M., Breunig, M. M., Kriegel, H.-P., & Sander, J. (1999). OPTICS: Ordering points to identify the clustering structure. In *ACM SIGMOD international conference on management of data* (pp. 49–60). ACM Press. https://www.researchgate.net/publication/221214752_OPTICS_Ordering_Points_to_Identify_the_Clustering_Structure

Arbitrum DAO. (2025). Sybil accounts: A conceptual overview. Available at: https://docs.arbitrum.foundation/concepts/sybil-account. Accessed 25 February 2025.

Arbitrum Foundation. (2023, March 16). $ARB airdrop eligibility and distribution specifications | Arbitrum DAO - Governance docs. *Arbitrum DAO*. https://docs.arbitrum.foundation/airdrop-eligibility-distribution. Accessed 25 February 2025.

Beosin. (2023, May 27). A closer look at the anti-Sybil mechanism under the arbitrum airdrop hype. Available at: https://beosin.com/resources/a-closer-look-at-the-anti-sybil-mechanism-under-the-arbitrum?lang=en-US. Accessed 25 February 2025.

Blondel, V. D., Guillaume, J. L., Lambiotte, R., & Lefebvre, E. (2008). Fast unfolding of communities in large networks. *Journal of Statistical Mechanics: Theory and Experiment, 2008*(10), 10008. https://www.researchgate.net/publication/1913681_Fast_Unfolding_of_Communities_in_Large_Networks. Accessed 25 February 2025

Boey, N. (2024, September 25). 50 biggest crypto airdrops: $26.6B in 'free money'. *CoinGecko*. https://www.coingecko.com/research/publications/biggest-crypto-airdrops. Accessed 28 February 2025.

Gitcoin. (2021, May 27). Deterring adversarial behavior at scale in Gitcoin Grants. Available at: https://medium.com/block-science/deterring-adversarial-behavior-at-scale-in-gitcoin-grants-a8a5cd7899ff. Accessed 25 February 2025.

Imperva. (2025) Sybil Attack. Available at: https://www.imperva.com/learn/application-security/sybil-attack/#:~:text=The%20name%20of%20this%20attack,Douceur%2C%20both%20at%20Microsoft%20Research. Accessed 25 February 2025.

Matsuoka, D., Lazzarin, E. (2024, October 16). Estimating the number of real crypto users. Available at: https://a16zcrypto.com/posts/article/estimating-crypto-users/#section%2D%2D1. Accessed 25 February 2025.

Messias, J., & Yaish, A., & Livshits, B. (2023). Airdrops: Giving money away is harder than it seems. https://doi.org/10.48550/arXiv.2312.02752. https://arxiv.org/pdf/2312.02752

Mocaverse. (2024). Claiming Your $MOCA Airdrop: Moca NFT | by Animoca Brands | Mocaverse. *Medium*. https://medium.com/mocaverse/moca-nft-airdrop-1f7e667911f1. Accessed 25 February 2025.

Passport XYZ. (2024, October 16). Passport XYZ Docs—Passport XYZ. https://docs.passport.xyz/. Accessed 25 February 2025.

Platt, M., & McBurney, P. (2023). Sybil in the haystack: A comprehensive review of blockchain consensus mechanisms in search of strong sybil attack resistance. *Algorithms, 16*(1), 34. https://doi.org/10.3390/a16010034. https://www.mdpi.com/1999-4893/16/1/34

Trusta Labs. (2023, September 21) Airdrop-Sybil-identification. Available at: https://github.com/TrustaLabs/Airdrop-Sybil-Identification. Accessed 25 February 2025.

Uniswap. (2020, September 1). How do I claim the Uniswap UNI Token Airdrop?" *Uniswap Labs*. https://support.uniswap.org/hc/en-us/articles/10794055772813-How-do-I-claim-the-Uniswap-UNI-Token-Airdrop. Accessed 25 February 2025.

Wormhole. (2024, May 11). From eligibility to Sybil detection: A deep-dive into Wormhole's multichain airdrop. Available at: https://wormhole.com/blog/from-eligibility-to-sybil-detection-a-deep-dive-into-wormholes-multichain. Accessed 25 February 2025.

Yu, H., Kaminsky, M., Gibbons, P., & Flaxman, A. (2006). SybilGuard: Defending against Sybil attacks via social networks. https://www.researchgate.net/publication/200110697_SybilGuard_defending_against_sybil_attacks_via_social_networks

Chapter 5
Blockchain Applications in Business Ecosystems

Paul Sin

5.1 Challenge of Blockchain Adoption

While the technology of blockchain is fascinating, business practitioners struggled at first to find real business use cases. "Real" refers to the ability of enterprises to justify the investment of building a blockchain infrastructure with a proper return. One of the barriers to blockchain adoption in the business world was its anonymity.

In the business world, all transactions comprise two legs: delivery versus payment. When you buy something, may it be a bottle of water or a lot of shares, the sellers will need to deliver the title of the goods to you, and simultaneously the buyer will need to pay the seller for the goods (or services). If both the buyer and seller are anonymous, it will be hard to enforce legal liability when one of them fails to fulfill their obligations. This risk is called counterparty risk.

During the early stage of blockchain development, counterparty risk is solved by irreversible and immutable atomic transactions embedded in smart contracts. These smart contracts are programming codes that are triggered by events. Therefore, when delivery happens, it will automatically trigger payment. This sounds perfect except that the payers and payees are both anonymous, hence blockchain with its cryptocurrency has become a great platform for money laundering and other criminal activities. That is why most cyberattacks, such as ransomware, will ask for bitcoins. Besides, if a person needs to launder money, he can also buy a non-fungible token (NFT) at one dollar from the person who holds the illegitimate funds and sell it back to that person at a million dollars, in order to create a source-of-fund proof and bank in the money. Of course this is a simplified version of what is happening today, but it explains why regulators are so concerned about blockchain, cryptocurrencies, and digital assets in general when they are transacted on an anonymous platform. The regulatory concerns in turn prohibit traditional financial institutions

P. Sin (✉)
Emali Global Inc., Canada, Montreal

Y. Xiong (ed.), *Blockchain Analytics for Practitioners*, Business Analytics in Practice, https://doi.org/10.1007/978-3-032-06046-4_5

and corporates in general from adopting blockchain and digital assets, until the emergence of permissioned blockchain.

5.2 Rise of Permissioned Blockchain

Permissioned blockchain, by the name of it, requires proper onboarding before users can access the platform. Unlike public blockchains such as Bitcoin and Ethereum networks, permissioned blockchains carry named users who have already done the know-your-customer (KYC) or know-your-member (KYM) processes instead of anonymous users. As a result, it is welcomed by many jurisdictions, especially the financial world. Hyperledger Fabric and R3 Corda are two of the more popular permissioned blockchains deployed in the business world.

In permissioned blockchains, transactions are digitally signed by named users, hence all the costly operations such as proof-of-work or gas payments can be eliminated. The performance can also be increased from a transaction every few minutes to thousands of transactions every second. The most important feature is its ability to attribute legal liability to the users, thus its ability to comply with regulatory requirements.

It has been a misunderstanding that permissioned blockchains compromise data privacy. Like public blockchains, permissioned blockchains also come with many Privacy Enhancing Technologies (PET), such as data hashing, zero-knowledge proof, etc. Users can safely exchange and synchronize sensitive data without being exposed to the rest of the community. Data analysis can also employ techniques such as differential privacy, federated analysis, homomorphic encryption, etc., to obtain insights from the platform while protecting data privacy. The fact that many permissioned blockchain platforms are cross-border implies their abilities to comply with the most stringent data privacy laws such as General Data Protection Regulation (GDPR) in European Union (EU) or China Personal Information Protection Law (PIPL).

There are a few drawbacks though. Permissioned blockchains are not readily deployed globally like Bitcoin or Ethereum networks. When an ecosystem decides to deploy a permissioned blockchain network, they will have to provision infrastructure resources such as data node hosting and network connectivity for the platform. Besides, the onboarding process will require a governance model, usually in the form of consortium or joint venture, to operate efficiently. The governance model will also need to take care of data standards, API standards, change and release management, etc. Therefore, it is in fact more costly to set up the network, leaving most networks in the hands of the large corporations instead of individual users.

Due to the nature of permissioned blockchain, it is more suitable for solving the "real" business problems, at least from the regulatory compliance perspective. There were many attempts and countless proof-of-concepts being done in the early stage of the blockchain adoption, notably with many failures. The successful cases

have one thing in common, they are trying to solve one and only one problem, i.e. B2B data synchronization.

5.3 Many-to-Many B2B Data Synchronization

Synchronizing data is a very common operation in the technological world. We synchronize emails every day from the company mail server to our mail clients, either installed on our mobile phone or our laptop computers. When we place orders on a mobile app, the order is captured in the app, then synchronized onto the server of the e-Commerce company. Similarly, when an insurance agent has captured the data of a new customer with the app installed in the tablet, the data will be synchronized back to the database of the insurance company. In these scenarios, blockchain is not required, instead the traditional client-server data exchange should suffice.

However, when an insurance company is selling policies through a bank partner, namely a bancassurance channel, the bank will capture the data in their own banking system instead of a software client provided by the insurance company. To synchronize data between the database sitting in the bank system and the insurance system, Open Application Programming Interface (API) can be deployed. API is basically a channel for two systems to exchange data, and Open API allows cross-organizational data exchanges in a secure manner. In this scenario, blockchain is again not required.

Blockchain, or permissioned blockchain to be specific, is required when it is a many-to-many B2B (Business-to-Business) data synchronization. If the data synchronization is B2C (Business-to-Customer) or B2E (Business-to-Employee), then client-server data exchange should be used. If the data synchronization is B2B but only one-to-one, or even many-to-one or one-to-many, then Open API should be used. There are many one-to-many use cases such as price data feeds. There are also many-to-one use cases such as regulatory data reporting, sending data to the same regulator. These use cases should use Open API. Only when the data synchronization is happening among multiple parties, for instance, importer, exporter and their banks involved in a letter of credit arrangement, or suppliers, retailers, logistics companies involved in a supply chain, then permissioned blockchain can be considered.

The distributed ledger technology (DLT) underlying permissioned blockchain basically operates in two steps: broadcast the data update and then achieve data consistency among all parties. Of course, there are also many other features to all blockchains, such as an immutable audit trail, autonomous smart contracts, data privacy protection, etc. However, the secured data synchronization among multiple parties has proven to be the key reason why some business ecosystem continues to invest in the platform while others pulled out after the hype of blockchain faded.

5.4 Use Case #1: Trade Finance

The first use case, also perhaps the most popular one, is trade finance. In this scenario, when a seller receives a purchase order (PO) from their customer, they will have to procure raw materials, labor, etc., so that they can fulfill the order. This will require working capital. The seller has an option to take the PO to the bank, proving that they have real business and the ability to pay back, if the bank can provide them with financing. Once the seller obtains the loan, they can produce the goods, get paid, and repay the bank with interest. This is also called open account financing. It does seem like a win-win situation and there should be no reason why the bank rejects the request.

Unfortunately, most banks would reject this kind of financing, leaving the seller with very expensive financing options, usually requiring the owner's personal guarantee also. The banks are concerned about a few risks. First, the PO presented could be fake. After all, it is just a piece of paper or facsimile. Second, the PO could be real, but the numbers are tampered with. Third, the seller may present this PO to multiple banks and obtain duplicated financing. You may be surprised to learn that these document fabricating and duplicated financing are in fact quite common. During COVID, an oil trading company in Singapore named Hin Leong Trading managed to owe 23 lenders $3.85 billion in total before it collapsed. Its owner Lim was charged with forgery and was sentenced to 17.5 years of jail (Khasawneh and Jaganathan, 2020).

To avoid these kinds of losses, banks tend to only finance companies they have been doing business with for decades, instead of small and medium enterprises (SME) and entrepreneurs. However, SME represents more than half of the employments in many developing countries and is the path for the uneducated poor to uplift themselves into middle class. Hence, many governments are very keen to support SME financing, usually under the banner of "financial inclusion."

What if we have a data synchronization platform that allows the bank to validate the authenticity of the PO presented by the seller with the buyer? If the buyer is a credible large enterprise, and the PO is digitally signed by them, then there is no reason why the bank should avoid financing the seller. If the platform keeps the PO data synchronized among all parties in the ecosystem, then the risk of tampering will be minimized. As a result, permissioned blockchain can effectively reduce the risk in trade and lower the cost of fund for sellers, especially SME, significantly. The last challenge is duplicated financing.

Fortunately, blockchain comes with one-way irreversible encryption, which allows encrypted PO to be synchronized to all participants on the platform without exposing sensitive customer information to the competitors. After the PO data is encrypted, everyone in the ecosystem will have a copy in their own data node. When the same PO is presented to another bank, through the same encryption, the same encrypted data will be generated and will have a collision. This is how duplicated financing are detected without compromising on data privacy protection. This also allows corporates and financial institutions to exchange sensitive data across borders, facilitating global trade digitization. That is why many organizations such as World Trade Organization (WTO) drives blockchain adoption.

With all these data captured by trade finance blockchain platforms, it will provide very useful information for customs, tax authorities, and even anti-money laundering (AML) investigations. For instance, Singapore Customs was among the first government bureau that drove one of the first blockchain adoptions in trade finance.

The vast data available in trade finance blockchain platforms will yield tons of useful analytics. Insurance firms are the first to discover this use case. They use the logistic data sitting on the platform to assess the risk of delivery and hence substantially lower the insurance premium. In the past, insurance firms had to assume the goods are constantly somewhere in the ocean, hence charge the seller at the highest premium to cover the risk. Now that the logistics firms can share the location of the goods through the blockchain platform, the underwriting of the risk can be much more precise, saving premiums for both the sellers and the buyers.

These use cases further lure additional participants to join the blockchain platform, leading to the rise of blockchain consortia. For instance, major carriers around the world such as COSCO Shipping, Hapag-Lloyd, CMA CGM, OOCL, the Port of Singapore Authority (PSA), etc., formed a joint venture named Global Shipping Business Network (GSBN, 2025) to amass and commercialize useful data captured from the global trade logistics. Data consumers, and financial institutions in particular, are very interested in subscribing to the data shared through blockchain platforms. At the end of the day, the key job of financial institutions is pricing risk. The more transparency they can obtain, the better they assess the risk, offer competitive pricing and avoid losses.

Similar data platforms are being established by governments, such as the Commercial Data Interchange (CDI) platform built by Hong Kong Monetary Authority (HKMA, 2024) or Dubai Trading Platform (Dubai, 2019) both enabled by blockchain. The CDI platform included e-commerce, logistics, telecommunication, etc., to provide useful information for banks to finance SME. This echoes back to the theme of financial inclusion advocated by many governments, especially during the COVID situation.

Many use cases have involved financial institutes to provide return on investment (ROI) and justify the building of the blockchain platform, but there are also blockchain platforms that are not supported by the financial services, notably the traceability platforms.

5.5 Use Case #2: Traceability and Sustainability

While trade finance or supply chain financing platforms are among the first to adopt blockchain technology, the most popular ones are probably traceability platforms. In places like Asia, counterfeit products are pervasive. Consumers can easily buy fake watches, fake handbags, fake food, fake car parts, fake wine, fake drugs and vaccines, etc., and these products certainly caused huge number of problems, from product safety to fatal poisoning.

How pervasive is counterfeit products? In January 30, 2023, a law enforcement taskforce raided a warehouse with 40,000 bottles of fake Penfolds, Lafite, etc., in Fujian, worth $150 million (Mustacich, 2023). A government official from China once said that at least half of the Lafite sold in China was fake (Qin, 2019). Lots of fake wines are not only fake, but they are also mixed with methanol and thus poisonous. Similarly, thousands of people were given fake vaccines in India during COVID, leaving them vulnerable to the pandemic with false security (Pathak, 2021).

To fight counterfeit, blockchain can provide a useful infrastructure. When the retailer claims that a bottle of wine is from Bordeaux, consumer can easily scan the QR code adhered to the bottle and see how the bottle was passed from a French cellar to a wholesaler, logistics companies, warehouse, and finally the retailer. The data at each checkpoint are uploaded and digitally signed by the corresponding ecosystem participants. This data cannot be tampered with because they are constantly synchronized among all parties in the supply chain through a permissioned blockchain. Any fake data will be rejected due to inconsistency.

However, there are two potential frauds in this design. First, if data are manually entered, then no matter how the blockchain synchronizes the data, the data will not be trustworthy. "Garbage in, garbage out," any garbage in blockchain is just immutable garbage but still not trustworthy. The second potential fraud, and perhaps the more challenging one, is the reliability of the QR code. If the counterfeit merchant can produce fake wine, they can certainly produce fake QR code, even when the QR code labels are holographic anti-counterfeit laser-print. Many other options are explored since then, including RFID, NFC, molecular identification tags, and many other forms of Internet-of-Things (IoT). For wine, owing to its high value, more advanced methods such as spectroscopic approach in combination with chemometrics are being employed (Ranaweera et al., 2021). Binding the physical products with the digital record on blockchain is called the problem of digital twins or the problem of the two chains.

There are many other products that require a solution to the digital-twin problem. Diamond traceability, one of the earliest use cases in blockchain space, will be very useful for eliminating stolen diamonds, resulting in lower insurance premiums for jewelers. Millions of diamonds are recorded on chain nowadays, together with their GIA certificates. Kimberley Process (KP) certification is also being uploaded on blockchain to avoid diamonds from conflict zones, also known as "blood diamonds." However, there is no reliable to bind the digital record with the physical product. It was not until laser engraving in diamond became possible, then the diamond can really be marked with a very small unique number, visible only under microscope, without compromising on its clarity.

Tracing continuous flow products such as oil and coal are more challenging. A coal importer once estimated that when a ship with coal passes through an Indian port, the weight of the coal will not change, but the quality will be reduced by 10%. Back in 2024, Adani Group was accused of buying low quality coal from Indonesia and selling them as high quality one, reducing not only the production efficiency of the power plant, but also the air quality and thus health of the population (McCrum et al., 2024). Trying to apply traceability network in this situation will encounter a big difficulty, i.e. how to tag the coal. One can always tag the container but there is nothing to prevent switching or diluting of the content during transportation. Smart containers can be a potential solution in this case.

A decade ago, there was a country which spent hundred million dollars to clear up illegal dumping of garbage to be recycled near the countryside, because the logistic contractors who were supposed to transport the garbage to recycle factories wanted to save the transportation cost, hence dumping the garbage midway. Tracing the garbage using IoT or any other tagging would mean throwing the tags away with the garbage, resulting in lots of waste and staggeringly high cost. Eventually, smart containers were used, and whenever the containers were opened midway or the weight of the content was reduced, the signal will be sent through Low-Earth Orbit (LEO) satellites to the blockchain. Data are then shared among all ecosystem participants and eliminated the loopholes of illegal dumping.

Similarly, when refrigerated containers or "reefers" are used to transport goods, such as wine or COVID vaccines that need to be stored at −90 °C to −60 °C, power is available for IoT also, and the condition of the cargos can be synchronized real-time through LEO satellites and blockchain real-time, ensuring the quality assurance of the goods throughout the shipment.

These use cases have inspired the deployment of many sustainability platforms. Seafood value chain, for instance, worked with Marine Stewardship Council (MSC) to upload "ecolabels" onto blockchain so that the whole supply chain can support sustainable fishing more effectively (Blaha and Katafono, 2020). Similarly, when agricultural products are being exported, the importers will also demand a Forest Stewardship Certificate (FSC), and it is much more trustworthy to have FSC signed and synchronized on blockchain than a piece of paper, potentially damaged or forged.

Lots of effort has been put into capturing carbon footprints too. IoT devices were installed at chimneys and electricity meters are all IoT-enabled. However, carbon footprints are not just generated by one company, but the whole supply chain. Therefore, supply chain blockchains are now used to capture emissions from the energy provider as well as the upstream and downstream suppliers, also called scope 2 and 3 emissions, respectively. Again, blockchain provides a trustworthy platform for data analytics sharing but the carbon data captured have to be authentic. If there are manual manipulations on the IoT devices or even the data themselves, then blockchain itself will not be able to improve data reliability and validity.

With sustainability platform in place, corporates and SME alike can try to hedge the carbon emissions with carbon credits, and the latter are increasingly available through blockchain-enabled carbon exchanges. Many tokenized carbon credits are backed by forest planted for the purpose, hence contributing to the reduction of greenhouse gas (GHG) effectively. Apart from regulatory requirements, this effort can sometimes generate financial returns through green bond issuance and can help lower cost of funds for corporates and their projects. Unfortunately, many banks are still in their early stages to justify lower pricing through sustainability certifications.

In short, when data on supply chain can be synchronized securely on blockchain for the whole ecosystem, including regulators, vast amounts of valuable data analytics will be generated for countless applications, from financing to insurance, anti-counterfeit, sustainability, etc. There are hundreds of blockchain platforms deployed for these purposes. Some are covering a horizontal ecosystem, such as all the logistics firms form a consortium and build a network like GSBN, others are covering a vertical one, such as tracing diamonds from diamond mine to jewelry shops.

5.6 Use Case #3: Central Bank Digital Currency (CBDC)

As of September 2024, there are three countries (The Bahamas, Jamaica, and Nigeria) launched and using Central Bank Digital Currency (CBDC), 44 piloting, and 59 countries in research and development stage. There are multiple motives behind this initiative. Some are driving CBDC for financial inclusion, especially in countries with large unbanked population and an unstable financial infrastructure. People in some countries lost confidence in their banks or even their central bank and government, resulting in uncontrollable inflation. Some countries are afraid of sanction and need a cross-border trade settlement platform alternate to the existing ones operated by a few oligopolies. To understand the phenomenon, CBDC must be properly defined first. In general, CBDC can be categorized by retail or wholesale, token-based or account-based, one-tier or two-tier, as well as domestic or cross-border.

5.6.1 Retail Versus Wholesale

The target users of retail CBDC is peer-to-peer payments, usually for countries with less developed financial infrastructure such as POS networks or with relatively large unbanked population. When people need to carry lots of cash to market for transactions, it is both inconvenient and unsafe. Retail CBDC can also be driven by a lack of confidence in the retail bank, forcing the central bank to step in and back the currency digitally.

Wholesale CBDC, on the other hand, targets traders, who need a way to securely and effectively settle their trades, due to the large transaction amount involved. Developed countries may have good Real-Time Gross Settlement (RTGS) systems for interbank settlement and B2B payments, but not the developing countries. When the settlement is not real-time, traders suffer from long cash days, tight liquidity and hence high cost of funds. Remittance through private platforms and liquidity providers can be costly too.

Regulators are also finding it difficult to enforce AML regulations, and any investigations will last for a few weeks before the release of funds, thus affecting the liquidity of the traders again. CBDC running on permissioned blockchain will significantly enhance the transparency of the remittance with underlying trade, as well as identify trade counterparts through the corresponding bank's know-your-customer (KYC) data uploaded on the platform, resulting in reduction of AML investigation effort. In some countries with currency control, such as China, proof of trade is required before foreign currency can be exchanged. The data on blockchain will become both handy and trustworthy for the purpose.

5.6.2 Token-Based Versus Account-Based

Whether CBDC should be token-based or account-based is more a technical question than a practical one. Simply said, token-based payment does not update balance upon sending or receiving payments, but carries the updated balance with each transaction, which is then synchronized to the whole network. This is the original design of Bitcoin network, allowing the flexibility of the owner to use different wallets simultaneously and assure his or her anonymity.

Account-based, on the other hand, requires an account identifier with an outstanding balance, which is updated every time after a transaction. Permissioned blockchain will be more suitable to implement such platform, with named users operating their corresponding accounts. As regulations are getting tighter and tighter globally, permissioned blockchain is becoming the default choice for central banks to implement CBDC networks.

5.6.3 One-Tier Versus Two-Tier

One-tier CDBC implies issuing of CBDC by the central bank directly to the end users, effectively by-passing commercial banks. This can be useful when the public lose faith in the commercial banks and start bank-runs. However, as central bank should not conduct lending and compete with commercial banks, the money deposited in the central bank CBDC accounts cannot be leveraged like commercial bank, essentially shrinking the liquidity in the market.

Two-tier CBDC implies injection of CBDC from the central bank to the commercial banks, and the commercial banks can then leverage the CBDC reserve to provide liquidity to the market. In this scenario, the money supply will not be affected, and the commercial banks can continue to compete on pricing and services, including the user experience of their digital wallets.

With its obvious advantages against one-tier CDBC, two-tier CBDC has been more widely adopted by major central banks particularly in developed countries. The data captured by this CBDC network and the analytics generated are very useful for the monitoring capital adequacy, predicting monetary flow, and formulating the fiscal policies.

5.6.4 Domestic Versus Cross-Border

When CBDC is used domestically, it can be used for peer-to-peer payments among the public, domestic remittance and interbank clearings. For the public, the value of a domestic payment platform depends on whether there are existing digital payment ecosystems. From the success of M-PESA in Africa to the one billion mobile payment users in China, using Alipay, WeChat Pay, or UnionPay every day, domestic peer-to-peer and B2C payment platforms are quite well established, leaving little gaps for CBDC to address. Regarding domestic remittance, in other words B2B payments, there are also an increasing number of FinTech companies challenging the traditional less efficient banking services. When the private sector is doing well, there is no reason why central banks should spend the taxpayer money to develop another platform. As for interbank clearing, lots of them were not real-time in the past, and day-end clearing often encounters dead-locks, which requires central bank to resolve. The last issue did engender some CBDC initiatives, such as Project Ubin (Monetary Authority of Singapore, 2024). However, more and more interbank clearing and settlement platforms are enhanced into a real-time platform. The RTGS nowadays no longer supports only big-ticket transactions but also smaller amounts at a relatively low cost. Together with the fast payment systems being deployed by many jurisdictions, the justification of building a domestic CBDC network is becoming very weak.

On the other hand, cross-border CBDC projects are now gaining momentum. Multiple central banks are collaborating to deploy multilateral CBDC networks. For instance, the Reserve Bank of Australia (RBA), Central Bank of Malaysia (BNM), MAS, and South African Reserve Bank (SARB) initiated Project Dunbar for international trade settlement. Bank of Thailand (BOT) and HKMA also started Project Inthanon Lionrock, and have evolved the platform into m-Bridge, adding in Central Bank of the UAE (CBUAE) and the People's Bank of China (PBOC). The ability of permissioned blockchain in supporting regulatory compliance while protecting data privacy renders it a perfect technology to enable cross-border data exchange, and payment is essentially a data exchange, with a few data items, including sender, receiver, time, and amount. Permissioned blockchain underlying these CBDC networks enables real-time cross-border remittance without heavy dependence on an infrastructure provided by a few dominating operators such as SWIFT.

While blockchain is a distributed ledger with decentralized data and file hosting, permissioned blockchain requires the deployment of some centralized components, such as key and credential management, member onboarding services, consensus mechanisms, etc. While multiple jurisdictions may agree to collaborate, they will still have concerns on hosting critical infrastructure in another foreign country. Therefore, one major roadblock is to resolve the trust issue lying among the collaborating central banks. This can only be resolved with more decentralized architecture, namely Web3, to be discussed next.

5.7 The Future: Evolution of Web3

The need for centralized components has prevented many blockchain proof-of-concept projects from launching into production. Many consortia end up forming a joint venture to align their interest, but not all ecosystem participants can join a joint venture, notably central banks. A new and more decentralized architecture is required if blockchain can be deployed in many real-world ecosystems.

There have been many definitions for Web3 since it became a catch-phase, and its essence is the deployment of a decentralized architecture without any technology giants running the core components, such as global software firms, cloud providers, or certificate authorities (CA). The first step is to adopt decentralized identity (DID) for all users. On one hand, the users are still named, but on the other hand they do not have to be onboarded by a centralized governance body. A government can issue digital identity for its own citizens, also known as the sovereign identity; a bank can issue digital identity for its customers, such as online banking credentials; a university can also issue digital identity for its graduates, with their transcripts. In society, many entities will possess lots of identity information. An individual can thus create his or her own DID, using all the other digital identities such as sovereign identity or online banking credentials as foundational identities to prove his or her authenticity. The more foundational identities the individual can incorporate, the more authentic and thus trustworthy the resulting DID is. This technique is also called social crafting.

With social crafting, an individual can issue his or her own keys for encryption and digital signing, without relying on a centralized CA. However, an ecosystem will need to approve which entities can provide trustworthy foundational identities first. These trusted entities will be broadcasted to the whole ecosystem through a decentralized record called Trust Registry (TR), a little bit similar to Domain Name Services (DNS) in the Internet today.

With DID, data can now be signed and exchanged upon consent from the users. Consent management is enabled with the Web3 DID wallet, which holds all the data. The wallet data can be a university transcript, bank account statement, tax return, credit score record, etc. When the wallet user gives consent to update the account balance and exchanges the information with another wallet to update the account balance of the recipient wallet, a typical payment transaction is conducted. Consent management is hence like the traditional mechanism of authorization. The last mile is the interoperability between this new way of payment authentication and authorization with the existing legacy payment infrastructure. Once the interoperability is solved, then the whole new Web3 economy without dependence on any dominating technology providers will be feasible.

Digital identity, authorization and consent, payment interoperability, and data exchange are the four main pillars of critical infrastructure for an inclusive digital economy (Monetary Authority of Singapore, 2021). The evolution from public blockchain, permissioned blockchain to web3 architecture has been a result of a decade's trial and error. With web3 architecture, the trade finance platform will find integrating highly regulated financial institutes with non-financial institutes easier, supply chain platforms will find building trust among cross-border participants easier, and central banks will find deploying infrastructure for multiple jurisdictions easier. After all, the network is now truly decentralized, without much need for deploying and hosting of centralized components.

Unfortunately, when all data are stored as fragments in decentralized wallets, blockchain analytics will be less readily available compared to permissioned blockchain. Consents will have to be obtained from all Web3 wallets before aggregated data can be derived from the network. A potential solution is to let an agent of Artificial Intelligence (AI) crawl through all wallets and train its neural network through machine learning. The agent may not be able to provide traditional descriptive statistics of an ecosystem but can provide inferences based on the insights learned from the network. In the future, a bank may be advised by an AI agent to finance a SME, without access to the underlying data. Nevertheless, the potential of integrating blockchain, particularly web3 network, with AI is yet to be actualized, and something really exciting to look forward to.

References

Blaha, F., & Katafono, K. (2020). Blockchain application in seafood value chains. *FAO Fisheries and Aquaculture Circular*, 1207. https://doi.org/10.4060/ca8751en. Retrieved April 1, 2025, from https://openknowledge.fao.org/server/api/core/bitstreams/e7401fd1-ee65-4523-9f42-abf874605427/content

Dubai Chamber. (2019). *Dubai trading platform—A Blockchain enabled trading platform*. Retrieved April 1, 2025, from https://www.wto.org/english/res_e/reser_e/04_a_khalil_haddad_dubai_trade_platform_case_study_presentation.pdf

GSBN. (2025). *About GSBN*. Retrieved April 1, 2025, from https://www.gsbn.trade/about-gsbn

HKMA. (2024). *Commercial data interchange (CDI)*. Retrieved April 1, 2025, from https://www.hkma.gov.hk/eng/key-functions/international-financial-centre/fintech/research-and-applications/commercial-data-interchange/

Khasawneh, R. & Jaganathan, J. (2020). *Singapore oil trader Hin Leong owes $3.85 billion to banks*. Retrieved April 1, 2025, from https://www.reuters.com/article/business/singapore-oil-trader-hin-leong-owes-3-85-billion-to-banks-sources-idUSL3N2C41ZF/

McCrum, D., Cook, C., & Reed, J. (2024). *Adani suspected of fraud by selling low-grade coal as high-value fuel*. Retrieved April 1, 2025, from https://www.ft.com/content/7451f2de-91fa-49f3-acb3-e83ab5c00eff

Monetary Authority of Singapore. (2021). *MAS report on critical infrastructure for an inclusive digital economy*. Retrieved April 1, 2025, from https://www.mas.gov.sg/news/media-releases/2021/mas-report-on-critical-infrastructure-for-an-inclusive-digital-economy

Monetary Authority of Singapore. (2024). *Project Ubin: Central bank digital money using distributed ledger technology*. Retrieved April 1, 2025, from https://www.mas.gov.sg/schemes-and-initiatives/project-ubin

Mustacich, S. (2023). *Counterfeit Lafite, Penfolds seized in $150 million fake wine bust*. Retrieved April 1, 2025, from https://www.winespectator.com/articles/counterfeit-lafite-penfolds-seized-in-150-million-fake-wine-bust

Pathak, S. (2021). *Thousands given fake vaccines through scam in India*. Retrieved April 1, 2025, from https://www.npr.org/2021/07/09/1014512227/thousands-given-fake-vaccines-through-scam-in-india

Qin, A. (2019). *A French wine from China? This $300 bottle is the real thing*. Retrieved April 1, 2025, from https://www.nytimes.com/2019/10/24/business/china-wine-long-dai-lafite.html

Ranaweera, K. R., et al. (2021). A review of wine authentication using spectroscopic approaches in combination with chemometrics. *Molecules, 26*(14), 4334. https://doi.org/10.3390/molecules26144334

Paul Sin A fintech and transformation leader with over 25 years of experience in IT management, consulting, and innovation—had led the Group Technology function at New World Development, overseeing digital transformation across property, retail, healthcare, and infrastructure sectors. Previously, he founded Deloitte's Asia-Pacific Blockchain Lab and led its FinTech consulting practice, pioneering enterprise blockchain adoption and digital finance strategies.

Chapter 6
Regulatory Considerations in Decentralised Finance

Binu Paul

6.1 Introduction

Decentralised Finance (DeFi) holds promise as one of the most impactful developments in the world of finance, having evolved rapidly in just under a decade.

Premised on blockchain technology, DeFi refers to a set of financial services and applications that operate without centralised 'trust' based systems—i.e., those that rely on traditional financial intermediaries such as custodians, brokers, and financial services providers, such as banks and insurance companies.

Instead, DeFi platforms leverage the power of technology and innovations such as smart contracts, decentralised applications (dApps), and cryptographic protocols to offer a range of services, similar to what is offered in the traditional world—such as lending and borrowing, exchanging/trading, payments, derivatives, etc. The important difference though is the lack of a need for intermediaries, particularly in the context of regulations and regulatory activity.

The DeFI sector has transformed from a niche concept in blockchain and cryptocurrency communities to a rapidly growing ecosystem worth billions of dollars (Uzougbo et al., 2024a, 2024b). This trend can be attributed to a number of factors that a range of stakeholders have found appealing, such as its promise of democratising financial services, lower barriers to entry, aspects of its distributed nature, etc. On that basis, there has been a rising trend in developers, entrepreneurs, investors, and regulators getting increasingly involved in this sector. However, the sector's rapid rise also raises important questions about matters such as regulation, adoption, safety and its longer term sustainability to support commercially viable business models.

B. Paul (✉)
SavvyKiwi Limited, London, UK
e-mail: binu.paul@savvykiwi.com

Y. Xiong (ed.), *Blockchain Analytics for Practitioners*, Business Analytics in Practice, https://doi.org/10.1007/978-3-032-06046-4_6

This article will explore the journey so far with DeFi, examining its evolution and adoption as well as the challenges it throws up from a regulatory perspective, as the sector continues to mature.

6.2 The Origin Story

For centuries, financial assets such as stocks, bonds, commodities, and real estate have been utilised to build wealth and manage financial risk.

Financial assets represent value based on ownership of, or claims on, future cash flows or income. Such assets appeal to investors as they typically offer a combination of income (through dividends or interest) and the potential for capital growth. Real world assets, such as property and gold are physical in nature and can be owned and used to generate wealth.

Such traditional assets are characterised by a number of features including their creation, storage, ownership, transfer, and trade / exchange. All such activities and their records are stored, typically, on centralised ledgers and are represented via various types of intermediaries who link the counterparties and provide the element of 'trust'.

Further, such assets are defined by the nature of their risk-return tradeoffs, including solutions or structures that enable the control of liquidity, access, capital growth, income generation, etc. As examples:

- Stocks and shares have tended to have higher potential returns accompanied by higher risk, relative to bonds which traditionally have offered more stability, but with lower returns
- Real estate assets can be less liquid than stocks and bonds
- Some commodities may be exclusively accessible to only wholesale or institutional investors

Traditional financial assets and their providers are typically subject to strict oversight by regulatory agencies and financial authorities to ensure transparency, fairness, and investor protection. As such, well-established legal and regulatory frameworks already exist in relation to the offer, trading, settlement, and taxation of these assets (Fein, 2010). Such assets, and the activities related to them, have been long-established and as such widely understood by investors, regulators, and law enforcement agencies.

6.3 Digital Assets

New digital technologies emerging in the latter part of the 1900s helped digitise the representation of, and activities related to, financial assets - such as trading platforms (for e.g., E-Trade) and money (for e.g., DigiCash) (Marshall, 2018).

Whilst these technologies introduced the idea of digitising assets, they continued to rely on centralised systems, in some cases needing more than one intermediary, to establish 'trust' between counterparties.

The rise of the Internet in the mid-90s enabled the ability to consume information 'remotely' (online). While this first version of the Internet was limited to consuming information online ('read-only'), the introduction of Web 2.0 technologies in the early to mid-2000s enabled 'interactions' remotely ('read' and 'write') (Bellucci et al., 2010)—leading to the advent and rise of social media platforms. Yet, the provision of these activities continued to be reliant on centralised systems controlled by individual entities, providing the element of 'trust'.

As such, financial assets, activities related to them and their providers continued to be subject to oversight by regulatory and financial authorities, under established regulatory frameworks.

6.4 Crypto Assets

Bitcoin, introduced in 2009, was the first fully 'decentralised' digital asset (Kaal, 2020).

Bitcoin's blockchain technology allowed for peer-to-peer transactions without the need for intermediaries, such as a government, a central bank, or any single entity. It was a breakthrough, using cryptographic techniques to resolve the challenge of exchanging value digitally in an environment of zero-trust, i.e., it enabled online interactions between anonymous parties without the reliance on any intermediaries, to establish 'trust'.

It is helpful context that Bitcoin's launch was the result of long-term socio-cultural trends, technological advancements, and experimentation over many decades. This could be traced back to the late 80 s and early 90 s—a period that saw the origins of the 'cypherpunk' movement (Anderson, 2022)—a grassroots response to the growing concerns about privacy, surveillance, and state control over information.

Within the above context - of not needing a centralised entity at its helm, consumer outcomes driven by software code and the a lack of recourse for consumers (given the immutable nature of how blockchain systems are designed)- it has been increasingly challenging to design fit-for-purpose regulatory frameworks. Blockchain-based systems offer alternatives to traditional financial products and services, but tracking, monitoring, and enforcement become more challenging than with traditional financial products and services (Cheng, 2018).

6.5 Decentralised Finance (DeFI)

It is within the context of Bitcoin and its growth trajectory as a prospective store of value and a medium of exchange that DeFI would eventually come into being.

A notable milestone in its journey was the creation of the Ethereum blockchain, in 2015. Ethereum, developed by a group of developers, introduced a new concept called 'smart contracts', which forms the backbone of DeFI applications.

'Smart contracts' essentially automate the process of how terms in an agreement are executed, using software code. As such they are often referred to as self-executing agreements or contracts. For online transactions, this becomes especially relevant. It provides a solution for parties transacting online in full anonymity to be able to trust the counterparty to deliver on their commitment.

This level of programmability combined with a built-in trust mechanism provides some unique alternatives to how traditional financial services and markets are structured and delivered. For instance, in the traditional world when transacting in shares, the two counterparties are reliant on an intermediary ensuring that the exchange of shares and reciprocal payment amounts are settled appropriately. In the DeFI sector, software code provides that function, by executing the exchange in a pre-determined, automated manner.

The above concept holds promise in potentially enabling significant improvements to traditional financial services business models, if not provide new and unique alternatives. Yet, as the sector grows in prominence, so does the complexity in relation to how the provision of these services and products can be monitored, assessed and be provided regulatory guardrails.

6.6 The Early Days

While the idea of decentralised financial services was theoretically possible from Ethereum's launch in 2015, it was not until a few years later that DeFi truly began to gain traction. The initial phase of DeFi experimentation focused on developing simple applications for lending, borrowing, and trading (Kitzler et al., 2023).

MakerDAO, launched in 2017 on the Ethereum blockchain, is widely considered the first true DeFi protocol, introducing the DAI stablecoin backed by collateralised debt positions rather than centralised reserves (Feng et al., 2024). This innovation demonstrated that complex financial instruments could exist in a truly decentralised manner, setting the stage for an uptick in the launch of DeFi applications.

MakerDAO, a decentralised autonomous organisation (DAO), facilitates the creation and management of the DAI stablecoin, a cryptocurrency whose value is pegged to the U.S. dollar. DAI was unique as it was not backed by a centralised entity, like a bank, but by collateral locked into smart contracts on the Ethereum blockchain (Feng et al., 2024). MakerDAO allowed users to create DAI by locking up Ether (ETH) as collateral, and borrowing against it. This marked the first major step towards a decentralised stablecoin, which would go on to play a crucial role in the broader DeFi ecosystem.

In 2017, the launch of the ERC-20 token standard helped catalyse DeFi's growth by providing a standardised framework for creating new tokens on the Ethereum network (Venkata Viswas Reddy et al., 2024). The ERC-20 standard made it easier for developers to create tokens that could be easily integrated into dApps (decentralised applications) and other DeFi projects. This laid the foundation for the rapid proliferation of DeFi projects in the years that followed.

Some of the projects launched during these early days include EtherDelta and 0x (2016), providing basic services such as exchange of digital assets, and Compound (2018), a lending and borrowing platform - all without the need for an intermediary. For example, Compound allowed users to lend their cryptocurrency and earn interest, or borrow digital assets by using their existing holdings as collateral. The platform's algorithmic interest rate model enabled interest rates to fluctuate based on the supply and demand of each asset in the market, with a view to providing more efficient lending and borrowing than traditional financial institutions.

6.7 Growth Phase

While DeFi protocols had existed for a few years prior, 2020 set off a period of explosive growth that saw the Total Value Locked (TVL) in DeFi protocols surge from under $1 billion in early 2020 to over $15 billion by September of that year (Durachman, 2024).

This growth was catalysed by several key developments:

6.7.1 Yield Farming

Yield farming, also known as liquidity mining, involves users providing liquidity to decentralised blockchain protocols in exchange for rewards, often in the form of native tokens. This mechanism incentivised users to lock up their assets in DeFi protocols, thereby increasing the liquidity of those platforms and boosting their growth. Notably, protocols like Compound introduced governance tokens (COMP) distributed to users based on their participation, creating new incentive mechanisms that attracted billions in capital (Cousaert et al., 2022). This incentivised many users to participate in Compound, following which the COMP token (its native token), became one of the most valuable tokens in the DeFi space. Other platforms, such as Uniswap, Sushiswap, and Yearn Finance, soon adopted similar strategies, further accelerating the growth of the DeFi ecosystem.

6.7.2 Automated Market Makers (AMMs)

Uniswap and similar protocols revolutionised token trading by replacing traditional order books with liquidity pools, democratising market-making and token exchange.

6.7.3 Composability

DeFi's 'money legos' approach allowed protocols to build upon each other, creating complex financial products through the combination of simpler components (Saengchote, 2021).

6.7.4 Liquidity Mining

Projects began offering tokens as rewards for providing liquidity, creating a powerful virtuous cycle that rapidly increased TVL across the ecosystem.

The growth of DeFi was further fuelled not only by the broader cryptocurrency market rally in 2020, led by Bitcoin reaching new highs, but also by the growing interest from institutional businesses to be involved in the digital assets sector.

DeFi's rapid growth continued into 2021, with the sector becoming an increasingly important part of the broader cryptocurrency and blockchain ecosystem (Durachman, 2024). Also, by this time mainstream traditional financial (TradFi) market providers like Visa and JP Morgan had started exploring and experimenting with the idea of integrating the concepts of decentralisation within their traditional activities.

A number of other trends followed.

After several instances of high-profile hacks and vulnerability exploits, DeFi protocols started implementing more rigorous security practices, such as formal verification and professional audits (Xue et al., 2023). Also, the rise of Layer 2 solutions, such as Optimism and Arbitrum, further helped address scalability challenges faced by Ethereum-based DeFi platforms - rising volumes of users had led to slower and more expensive transactions. The objective of these solutions was the provision of faster and cheaper transactions while maintaining the security and decentralisation of the Ethereum network. Consequently, DeFi grew beyond Ethereum, with separate ecosystems developing on Solana, Avalanche, Binance Smart Chain, and such other Layer-1 blockchains.

Late 2021 saw the start of a sell-off in the broader crypto sector, which had a knock-on impact on the momentum in the growth of the DeFi sector as well. The following couple of years were marked by some high-profile failures, scams, and frauds, notable among them being the collapse of Terra/Luna, a Layer-1 blockchain designed to enable a stablecoin ecosystem. Some estimates put the decline in total locked value in DeFi protocols at around 75%, over this period (Liu et al., 2023).

Importantly, financial regulators began paying increasingly more attention to developments in the digital assets and crypto sector—especially given the rise of both consumer adoption of digital assets and the increasing interest from traditional financial providers looking to integrate the concepts of decentralisation into their mainstream activities. As such, policymakers in many jurisdictions began developing frameworks to address DeFi's regulatory challenges, signalling both its legitimisation and its potential constraints.

6.8 Here and Now

Today the DeFi sector has relatively matured, as indicated by a number of metrics.

While TVL took a significant hit over 2022–2023, as noted above, it has since recovered to now stand at $80–$100 billion, as at the start of 2025—noting it has grown from about $1 billion less than 5 years ago (Durachman, 2024). In the meanwhile, the number of unique addresses interacting with DeFi protocols has grown from a few thousand early adopters to millions of users worldwide. Decentralised exchanges (DEXs) now regularly process billions in daily trading volume - in some instances rivalling centralised exchanges (Lukianchuk, 2024).

Other indicators of a pick-up in momentum can be traced as per the developer activity on DeFi projects and interactions on community forums such as GitHub, with some of the leading protocols now generating significant revenue, and producing hundreds of millions in annual fees.

Within the above context, regulatory agencies around the globe continue to be challenged on how best to respond to these dynamic and fast evolving trends, two notable ones being the following:

6.8.1 Tokenisation of Real-World Asset (RWA) Assets

The tokenisation of real-world assets represents perhaps the largest opportunity for DeFi applications, potentially unlocking trillions in previously illiquid assets (Lukianchuk, 2024). From government bonds to real estate, art, intellectual property, and carbon credits, bringing these assets on-chain could dramatically expand DeFi's total addressable market as well as a significant shift in how these assets can be accessed, exchanged, and managed.

6.8.2 *The Convergence of DeFi and TradFi*

Major financial institutions have begun offering DeFi-inspired products, while DeFi protocols increasingly incorporate compliant on/off ramps and identity solutions. The increased involvement of institutional players in the DeFi sector will likely raise the stakes for regulators.

Traditional financial institutions operate within well-established regulatory frameworks, but the introduction of DeFi protocols challenges existing laws, especially regarding cross-border transfers and decentralised governance structures. The boundaries between DeFi and TradFi are blurring, with emerging hybrid models that combine DeFi's efficiency and transparency with TradFi's regulatory compliance and stability. In that light, regulators will increasingly face pressure to establish clearer guidelines for institutional participation in DeFi. Particularly so in relation to compliance with anti-money laundering (AML) and know-your-customer (KYC) regulations, tax reporting, and market surveillance.

As institutional capital continues to flow into DeFi, regulatory bodies will need to find a balance between fostering innovation and ensuring that good regulatory objectives, such as consumer protection, market integrity, competition etc., are achieved.

6.9 Challenges Faced by Financial Regulators in the DeFi Sector

Regulatory agencies are administrators who execute policy, the final design of which is enshrined within policy-making agencies.

In that context, at a policy level, the ruling Government's posturing will have a significant impact. Additionally, regulatory agencies operate with both scope constraints and resource constraints. This is relevant context for how regulators respond to events and trends, not only in their domestic market but also to trends internationally that affect their citizens (given the jurisdiction-agnostic nature of technology).

Regulations in relation to the wider crypto sector vary widely between jurisdictions and largely lack a consistent global approach. Some jurisdictions have created reasonably clear frameworks dedicated to this sector. Some others have extended beyond, or in absence of legislative clarity, taken on an enforcement-led approach, outright bans or taken an inconsistent stance. Whereas, there are a number of other countries who do not currently have any specific regulations targeted at the crypto sector.

Typically, financial regulators have the following objectives:

- Market integrity and efficiency
- Financial crime risk and
- Consumer / investor protection and outcomes (including competition)
- Financial stability

The rise of financial technology and digitisation added a new objective—to 'enable innovation' within the financial services sector, as many financial regulators also have a market development mandate.

Balancing these mandates with traditional regulatory objectives has proven challenging (Brummer & Yadav, 2017), as creating regulations to achieve those objectives can often delay or stifle innovation, and can lead to particular regulatory uncertainty.

This uncertainty is magnified especially at times of transition of the ruling powers and often hard to predict given the shifts in geo-politics over time. Regulatory agencies are only responsible for executing policy, the content of which often depend on the policy goals of the government in power. Political changes (such as the change in regime in the USA following elections in 2024) as well as geopolitical events add further uncertainty to the regulatory landscape as applicable to this sector.

Moreover, some jurisdictions have multiple regulatory agencies operating within the same sector, each with their own regulatory objectives. Unlike the traditional asset sectors where different regulatory agencies have clear and established division of responsibilities, the nascent nature of the cryptocurrency sector means that multiple regulatory agencies are often still trying and testing their own optimal regulatory approach and scope, sometimes resulting in overlapping or even conflicting regulatory impact. This challenge is exacerbated by the decentralised and borderless nature of cryptocurrencies, complicated by jurisdictional boundaries and creating ambiguity in enforcement mechanisms (Lee & Lheureux, 2020). Furthermore, scholars argue that the lack of a unified governance framework contributes to inefficiencies and potential conflicts among regulators, as seen in case studies such as the Bitcoin scaling debate and Ethereum hard forks.

Facing these competing priorities, regulators are often required to take on a fine balancing act. This tension almost invariably forms the backdrop of regulatory considerations. This means that, in practice, regulators do not always have a clear, definitive or consistent regulatory approach.

When it comes to DeFi structures, these complexities are magnified even more so, given some of the unique characteristics of the sector, which create significant challenges in fulfilling regulatory objectives and mandates.

The next section looks at the issues through the lens of three foundational regulatory activities—licensing, supervision, and enforcement.

6.10 Tackling Anonymity and Pseudonymity

DeFi, by its very design, eliminates centralised intermediaries and operates in a pseudonymous environment where users transact under cryptographic addresses rather than verified identities (Makarov & Schoar, 2022). This makes it difficult for regulators to track issuers, monitor the flow of funds, and detect illegal activity.

Traditional financial regulations typically focus on identifiable entities, such as banks, investment firms, exchanges, and other intermediaries. These entities are required to implement Know-Your-Customer (KYC) and Anti-Money Laundering (AML) procedures to verify the identity of their customers and detect illicit activities such as money laundering or terrorist financing. As such, these entities serve as regulatory toll gates, including having to maintain capital reserves, ensuring consumer protections, etc. (Ali, 2024).

Thus, a major challenge for regulators in the DeFi sector is the anonymity or pseudonymity that is built into many blockchain networks. While this feature is often touted as one of the key benefits of blockchain technology, it creates a significant hurdle for regulators tasked with monitoring financial transactions and ensuring compliance with financial laws (Makarov & Schoar, 2022). This absence of clearly regulatable entities undermines the traditional regulatory approach to licensing, supervision, and enforcement.

For example, decentralised exchanges (DEXs) allow users to trade assets without revealing their identity. While the transactions themselves are recorded on a public ledger, the participants remain pseudonymous, as blockchain addresses do not directly correlate to real-world identities. This creates a significant challenge for regulators who rely on KYC/AML measures to ensure that financial activities are transparent and compliant with national and international laws. For instance, with no centralised entity monitoring transactions, there is no obvious entity to take responsibility for identifying and reporting suspicious activities.

For the very same reasons, being the anonymity afforded by DeFi platforms, they are also exploited by bad actors, including money launderers, terrorists, and fraudsters, who can use these platforms to move illicit funds across borders with minimal oversight. Although some DeFi platforms are beginning to integrate KYC measures, the decentralised and pseudonymous nature of the ecosystem makes it difficult to enforce such policies consistently across the sector.

So, the fundamental regulatory challenge remains DeFi's foundational principle of permissionless access.

6.11 Tracking Borderless Activities

Another vexing challenge for regulators is the lack of international alignment with their counterparts when it comes to licensing, supervising, and enforcing laws.

DeFi platforms are inherently global, with users and other stakeholders spread across multiple jurisdictions, as such often lacking a clear geographical footprint. Whereas, traditional financial institutions typically operate within specific national borders and are subject to local regulations.

As discussed previously, many jurisdictions approach the regulation of this sector differently, often shaped by varying combinations of aspirations of the ruling Govt., access to resources, capability, and geo-politics. This makes cross-border regulation in the DeFi space very complicated, and this level of regulatory fragmentation creates uncertainty for the participants in the sector, as they navigate a patchwork of regulations that change over time.

In the absence of a unified regulatory framework, it is common for a single DeFi project to be subject to different rules depending on the jurisdiction of its users. For example, a DeFi protocol that facilitates exchange of digital assets could be considered a regulated financial service in one country but entirely unregulated in another or lightly regulated.

Even assuming that regulators are able to monitor overseas activities of DeFi platforms, the border-agnostic nature of the technology makes enforcement near impossible given the extraterritorial nature of offending, as local laws likely won't apply. This creates a situation where bad actors are able to exploit regulatory loopholes and conduct illicit activities from jurisdictions with weak or in some cases, no regulations.

6.12 Designing Standardised Classifications

Traditional financial markets have been established over centuries of activities and founded on established regulatory frameworks. As such, the artefacts that make up those markets are clearly defined and classified. Such classifications allow for consistency when it comes to how they are governed and regulated. Existing regulatory frameworks are well-established as a result.

When it comes to the DeFi sector, there are no clear-cut classifications. In the DeFi world, especially given its relative novelty and rapid evolution, there still remains legal ambiguity in relation to its products, services, and structures (Uzougbo et al., 2024a, 2024b). This is primarily due to its foundational elements such as anonymity, border-agnostic operations, immutability, programmability, and composability.

Here are three examples.

- A DeFi lending and borrowing protocol—this may very well blend elements of multiple activities such as banking, exchange, and custody.
- Tokens that confer governance rights over protocols—these combine elements of both securities and utilities.
- Liquidity provision to decentralised exchanges—these may constitute an investment activity potentially subject to securities regulation.

As such, there is a blurring of lines between classes of regulatable activities (as defined by traditional financial markets)—all that in a decentralised environment without an obvious responsible entity backing it. Traditional rules that apply to centralised financial institutions or companies simply do not fit the decentralised ethos of DeFi platforms, where decision-making is often distributed and not tied to any single entity.

Not only does such regulatory uncertainty affect both providers and users but regulatory gaps can be an open invitation for market abuse and fraud, as discussed in the next section.

6.13 Influencing Consumer / Investor Outcomes

In the traditional sense, financial regulators rely heavily on the disclosure obligations imposed on providers to report regularly on their products, services, and customers.

A key foundational element of DeFi is indeed its open-source nature and transparency, given that all transactions are recorded on publicly viewable blockchains (Makarov & Schoar, 2022). Ironically though, the reality is that while there is unprecedented technical transparency on blockchains by its very design and architecture, few users possess the technical expertise to assess the integrity of a smart contract, for example. Even otherwise, no one entity bears an obvious legal responsibility to provide timely, fulsome, and accurate disclosure to users.

Additionally, smart contracts being software code are prone to suffer from security vulnerabilities (Chu et al., 2023), but again, with no obvious entity responsible for the platform, users do not have recourse in instances where things go wrong. This is especially important to note, given the foundational feature of immutability on blockchains—once executed, blockchain transactions cannot be reversed, even in cases of fraud or error (Darvishi et al., 2024). Even in the face of a loss users have no recourse, unlike when dealing with traditional financial services where the licensed entity providing the product or service can be held liable and pursued for making good any losses.

To make things more challenging, the feature of composability adds more layers of complexity for regulators, whereby cross-chain activities and the interlinkages between various protocols make monitoring and assessing inherent risks much more difficult than traditional practices.

Not surprisingly, the DeFi sector (as well as the wider crypto ecosystem) has been beset with numerous high-profile frauds, scams, and instances of market manipulation. Many of these issues stem from the relative ease with which bad actors can launch DeFi projects without proper guardrails.

For instance, without a centralised entity or a regulator overseeing its operations, DeFi platforms can be susceptible to pump-and-dump schemes, where the price of a digital asset on an exchange platform is artificially inflated (via social media promotions, etc.), and then quickly sold off for profit by the developers.

Scams such as 'rug pulls' also thrive in the DeFi ecosystem as the anonymity provided proves to be a safe haven for malicious actors, whereby developers of a DeFi project abruptly withdraw liquidity from the platform, leaving investors with worthless tokens. These types of scams have become increasingly common as more inexperienced investors are drawn to the high returns promised by DeFi projects. As the developers are simply unidentifiable online actors, the recourse for users who are scammed is limited and so is the ability for regulatory agencies to intervene (Trozze et al., 2023).

In short, the level of opacity on DeFi platforms can lead to a lack of accountability and as such encourage fraudulent activities. Without the appropriate guardrails, such platforms can be prone to market manipulation and abuse.

6.14 Considerations for Financial Stability and Contagion

The increasing involvement of institutional players in the DeFi ecosystem will likely raise the stakes for regulators, even further.

DeFi is expected to continue attracting capital and participation from institutional investors. Traditional players such as hedge funds, pension funds, and traditional asset managers may engage in DeFi protocols to access higher yields, diversify portfolios, and hedge against inflationary pressures.

In the meantime, DeFi projects continue to forge ahead with the tokenisation of real-world assets, derivatives, and decentralised insurance with institutions starting to recognise the efficiency and cost-saving potential of DeFi protocols. As the integration between traditional financial institutions and DeFi protocols increases and as more hybrid models emerge, it will put increasing pressure on regulators from the perspective of the unique risks inherent within the DeFi ecosystem seeping into the traditional financial world.

While, on one hand, DeFi has the potential to be innovative in its offering to consumers as well as in promoting financial inclusion, it also presents potential systemic risks that threaten the stability of the broader financial system (Bekemeier, 2022), especially if the rate of consumer and institutional adoption continues to keep pace or accelerate.

6.15 Regulatory Pathways

Many regulators already adopt a 'technology-neutral' approach to designing regulatory frameworks, instead focussing on the underlying economic substance and related activities (Uzougbo et al., 2024a, 2024b). For example, a platform that provides loans, whether on a DeFi structure or on a traditional platform, provides the same service—lending. As an extension of this logic, the approach is one of 'same risk, same regulation'.

While such an approach may appear logical and could apply to parts of the crypto sector, it is likely not going to suit the nuances of DeFi and some of its unique foundational aspects. Rather than applying traditional regulatory frameworks to DeFi projects, regulators will need to consider more flexible, technology-specific regulations that account for the decentralised nature of these platforms.

Successful regulatory approaches will require core consumer protections while accommodating DeFi's unique architecture and potential benefits. While that may seem obvious, it is challenging to implement. Regulators will need to consider one or many of the options listed below.

6.16 Matching Technology Innovation

One alternative is for innovations in regulation to match the innovations that DeFi represents in the financial sector.

Considering that the fundamental tenet of DeFi is a borderless, code-driven environment, regulation itself may need to adopt such an approach. Regulation as code is already a concept that is being explored and some progress made.

For example, the Ethereum-based ERC-3643, also known as the Regulated Token Standard, previously known as the T-REX protocol, is an open-source suite of smart contracts that enables the issuance, management, and transfer of permissioned tokens. These tokens are typically subject to compliance requirements such as Know-Your-Customer (KYC) checks and anti-money laundering (AML) regulations. This type of standardisation to aid in regulatory compliance in tokenised assets ensures that token issuers and operators can meet legal obligations while maintaining the benefits of utilising blockchain technologies. Thus far, about $28bn worth of assets have been tokenized through ERC-3643.

Additionally, there is potential for regulators to innovate by leveraging new and emerging technologies, such as Artificial Intelligence (AI), that help identify decentralised transactions, track and monitor illegal activities like market manipulation and money laundering as well as assess DeFi activities using blockchain analytics tools. Adopting such initiatives will broaden the toolkit for regulatory agencies to help address some of the specific and unique risks posed by DeFi.

6.17 Cross-Border Regulatory Collaboration

In order to effectively regulate activities within the DeFi sector, given its borderless operational model, regulators will require unprecedented collaboration with their counterparts globally.

Regulators have the opportunity to design new and innovative DeFi specific regulatory frameworks and seek harmonisation of regulatory standards to address the challenges posed by cross-chain DeFi (Silvers, 2020). This can be enabled via international forums such as the International Organization of Securities Commissions (IOSCO) and the Financial Action Task Force (FATF).

The same goes for constructive engagement with the DeFi community both local and overseas.

As the interconnectedness between DeFi and traditional finance increases, regulators will need to develop specialised expertise in blockchain technology, smart contracts, and decentralised governance mechanisms. This will require agencies to attract, train, and retain talent with technical knowledge of these areas and work closely with blockchain developers and industry participants. Effective collaboration should help not only with internal capability building within regulatory agencies, but also enable a first-hand insight into the opportunities and challenges of fast evolving technology trends.

Working alongside industry participants can also lead to developing self-regulatory frameworks and standards for DeFi platforms, such as best practices for smart contract security, code review processes, developing guidelines for transparency and governance, and creating mechanisms for dispute resolution.

6.18 Conclusion

The adoption of blockchain technology, smart contracts, and dApps has helped individuals and businesses to access a wide array of financial services outside the traditional financial services systems. Over time, DeFi is likely to evolve into a more interconnected ecosystem, where assets and data can seamlessly move between various blockchain networks. But, as much as DeFi has unleashed the unprecedented potential for fundamentally transforming the financial services sector, it clearly will continue to have a number of headwinds to weather, including concerns around security, adoption, and regulations.

From a regulatory perspective, the key challenge is finding the balance that effectively addresses the risks, without being too restrictive for innovation that makes DeFi potentially transformative. To expect this balance to be constant is unrealistic. It will continue to shift as technologies mature and as regulators develop a deeper understanding of decentralised systems. The long-term success and integrity of the DeFi ecosystem will come from being able to develop a tailored and flexible regulatory approach.

Clearly, regulators have a crucial role to play in shaping the future of DeFi.

References

Ali, A. (2024). Decentralized finance (DeFi) and its impact on traditional banking systems: Opportunities, challenges, and future directions. *SSRN Electronic Journal*. https://doi.org/10.2139/ssrn.4942313

Anderson, P. (2022). Of Cypherpunks and Sousveillance. *Surveillance & Society, 20*(1), 1–17. https://doi.org/10.24908/ss.v20i1.14322

Bekemeier, F. (2022). Deceptive assurance? A conceptual view on systemic risk in decentralized finance. In: *Proceedings of the 2021 4th international conference on blockchain technology and applications*. ICBTA 21.

Bellucci, A., Malizia, A., & Diaz, P. (2010). The anatomy of web 2.0: The web as a platform to promote users' participation and collaboration. In *Quality and communicability for interactive hypermedia systems: Concepts and practices for design*. IGI Global.
Brummer, C., & Yadav, Y. (2017). The Fintech trilemma. *SSRN Electronic Journal*. https://doi.org/10.2139/ssrn.3054770
Cheng, A. (2018). Crypto-currency: Implication for regulatory governance. In *Proceedings of the 39th international academic conference, Amsterdam*. https://doi.org/10.20472/iac.2018.039.008
Chu, H., Zhang, P., Dong, H., Xiao, Y., Ji, S., & Li, W. (2023). A survey on smart contract vulnerabilities: Data sources, detection and repair. *Information and Software Technology [online], 159*, 107221. https://doi.org/10.1016/j.infsof.2023.107221
Cousaert, S., Xu, J., & Matsui, T. (2022). SoK: Yield aggregators in DeFi. In: *2022 IEEE international conference on blockchain and cryptocurrency*. IEEE.
Darvishi, I., Asare, B.T., Musa, A., Yeboah-Ofori, A., Oseni, W., & Ganiyu, A. (2024). *Blockchain technology and vulnerability exploits on smart contracts* (pp.160–167). https://doi.org/10.1109/ficloud62933.2024.00032
Durachman, Y. (2024). Blockchain and the evolution of decentralized finance navigating growth and vulnerabilities. *Journal of Current Research in Blockchain [online], 1*(3), 166–177. https://doi.org/10.47738/jcrb.v1i3.20
Fein, M. L. (2010). Dodd-frank act: Implications for securities activities of banks and their affiliates. *SSRN Electronic Journal*. https://doi.org/10.2139/ssrn.1657637
Feng, Z., Mohanty, H., & Krishnamachari, B. (2024). Modeling and analysis of crypto-backed over-collateralized stable derivatives in DeFi. *Frontiers in Blockchain, 7*. https://doi.org/10.3389/fbloc.2024.1392812
Kaal, W. A. (2020). *Digital asset market evolution* (Vol. 46, p. 910). Journal of Corporation Law.
Kitzler, S., Victor, F., Saggese, P., & Haslhofer, B. (2023). Disentangling decentralized finance (DeFi) compositions. *ACM Transactions on the Web, 17*(2), 1–26. https://doi.org/10.1145/3532857
Lee, J., & Lheureux, F. (2020). A regulatory framework for cryptocurrency. *SSRN Electronic Journal*. https://doi.org/10.2139/ssrn.3523862
Liu, J., Makarov, I., & Schoar, A. (2023). Anatomy of a run: The terra luna crash. *SSRN Electronic Journal*. https://doi.org/10.2139/ssrn.4426941
Lukianchuk, D. Y. (2024). Decentralized finance: Principles of functioning, infrastructure, risks. *Business Inform, 3*(554), 289–304. https://doi.org/10.32983/2222-4459-2024-3-289-304
Makarov, I., & Schoar, A. (2022). Cryptocurrencies and decentralized finance (DeFi). *SSRN Electronic Journal*. https://doi.org/10.2139/ssrn.4104550
Marshall, J. (2018). A nescient investment. *The Texas Orator*. https://doi.org/10.15781/t2pg1j57q
Saengchote, K. (2021). Where do DeFi Stablecoins go? A closer look at what DeFi composability really means. *SSRN Electronic Journal*. https://doi.org/10.2139/ssrn.3893487
Silvers, R. (2020). Cross-border cooperation between securities regulators. *Journal of Accounting and Economics, 69*(2–3), 101301. https://doi.org/10.1016/j.jacceco.2020.101301
Trozze, A., Davies, T., & Kleinberg, B. (2023). Of degens and defrauders: Using open-source investigative tools to investigate decentralized finance frauds and money laundering. *Forensic Science International: Digital Investigation, 46*, 301575–301575. https://doi.org/10.1016/j.fsidi.2023.301575
Uzougbo, N. S., Ikegwu, C. G., & Adewusi, A. O. (2024a). Regulatory frameworks for decentralized finance (DeFi): Challenges and opportunities. *GSC Advanced Research and Reviews [online], 19*(2), 116–129. https://doi.org/10.30574/gscarr.2024.19.2.0170
Uzougbo, S., Ikegwu, G., & Adewusi, A. O. (2024b). International enforcement of cryptocurrency laws: Jurisdictional challenges and collaborative solutions. *Magna Scientia Advanced Research and Reviews, 11*(1), 068–083. https://doi.org/10.30574/msarr.2024.11.1.0075
Venkata ViswasReddy, M.C., Charan Reddy, V.S., Rao, G.J. and Devi, N.R. (2024). Efficient token transfer using ERC-20 decentralized exchange. In: *2024 International Conference on Intelligent Systems for Cybersecurity (ISCS)*. Gurugram (pp. 01–06).

Xue, Y., Fan, D., Su, S., Fu, J., Hu, N., et al. (2023). A review on the security of the Ethereum-based DeFi ecosystem. *Computer Modeling in Engineering & Sciences, 139*(1), 69–101. https://doi.org/10.32604/cmes.2023.031488

Binu Paul A leading fintech and digital assets expert with over 25 years of experience in funds management, financial technology, and regulation across the UK, New Zealand, and India. As the former Head of Digital Assets at the UK's Financial Conduct Authority and the Specialist Lead FinTech at the Financial Markets Authority in New Zealand, he has played a pivotal role in shaping blockchain regulation, fintech policy, and technology-driven innovation strategies in financial services.

Chapter 7
Web 3.0, AI, and the Passion Economy

Utkarsh Amitabh

Doing what you love has been a pipedream for most people. "Passion economy" refers to the economic and cultural trend where people build a portfolio of careers working on things they are intrinsically curious about (Amitabh, 2023b). The phrase was coined by Adam Davidson, a reporter at NPR, and Li Jin, a former investor at Andreessen Horowitz, who quit her job to create her own VC fund. Unbeknownst to each other, both Adam and Li were studying how people were reshaping the world of work with the help of new technology platforms (Currier, 2021; Polischuk & Gershfeld, 2022). There was a clear schism between the gig economy popularized by the "Uber for X" model and the creative economy. Let us explore why.

7.1 The Creativity–Productivity Schism

For a long time, there was a perceived conflict between creativity and productivity, with those pursuing creative careers struggling financially. However, this is now changing. Gig workers are increasingly seeking more purposeful ways to earn a living, marking the rise of the passion economy and side gigs.

New platforms are allowing creators to monetize their talents and focus on what they love. The Internet is not only shaping culture but also revolutionizing the way we work. Even professionals in traditional roles are leaving their full-time jobs to participate in the passion economy. Generation Z creators, influencers, and investors are making different career choices compared to previous generations. This shift is reflected in how they learn, work, and earn, with creativity and productivity no longer viewed as opposing forces. Both are integral to the new creator ecosystem

U. Amitabh (✉)
University of Oxford, Oxford, UK
e-mail: utkarsh.amitabh.dphil@said.oxford.edu

Y. Xiong (ed.), *Blockchain Analytics for Practitioners*, Business Analytics in Practice, https://doi.org/10.1007/978-3-032-06046-4_7

emerging in Web 3.0, a decentralized and distributed Internet that we will explore further in this chapter.

While gig economy jobs once made creativity more standardized, they offered limited job security and hourly pay that often fell below minimum wage. Despite their importance, these jobs were often lacking in personal satisfaction, meaning, and career growth. Gig workers, many of whom worked longer hours than investment bankers or top engineers, were left struggling to make a decent income (Amitabh, 2023b).

The passion economy is growing because it provides innovative ways to earn money, achieve professional fulfillment, and access new career opportunities. This new economy will lead to the separation of work from traditional employment. People are now more likely to build a portfolio of passions that can generate income, allowing them to turn their passions into a sustainable career on their own terms. As the barriers to switching jobs decrease, people are finding new opportunities based on their reputation and demonstrated skills.

A clear example of how work is being unbundled from traditional employment is the story of Lebanese philosophy professor Mahmoud Rasmi, who left his university position to create cohort-based online courses. Although he had a passion for teaching philosophy, Rasmi found that the university system in Lebanon did not support his professional development. Now, he designs unique philosophy courses and uses Network Capital to host, sell, and promote his work. Within just a few months, he is earning thousands of dollars per month. Given Lebanon's ongoing economic and political challenges, Rasmi is among the few in the country who are generating a respectable income, all thanks to the passion economy (Amitabh, 2022).

Another example is Vicky Bennison, who initially studied zoology in college before earning an MBA from the University of Bath. She then worked in international development, spending time in regions such as Siberia, South Africa, and Turkmenistan. Today, she is widely recognized for creating *Pasta Grannies*, a YouTube channel where she films authentic Italian grandmothers (nonnas) preparing traditional handmade pasta.

7.2 Passion Economy and Web 3.0: A Historical Analysis

The first phase of the web, known as Web 1.0, revolved around how we access and consume information. Companies like Yahoo, Netscape, Craigslist, and AOL were central to this era. Google emerged as the dominant force by democratizing information and creating a profitable, advertisement-driven business model around it.

Web 2.0, the second era of the Internet, introduced platforms that fostered interaction, leading to the rise of Facebook, Instagram, Twitter, Reddit, LinkedIn, and others. This era saw information, goods, and services converge under unified platforms. People began to engage in activities like taking ridesharing cabs, booking trips, going on dates, and forming work connections with strangers. For example, Uber allowed users to hail rides or earn extra income by driving after work, while

Instagram turned content creation and video watching into everyday activities. The term "influencer" became established as a noun rather than a verb.

The defining feature of Web 2.0 was the peer-to-peer (P2P) exchange of information, which fueled the Internet's growth. However, the economic rewards largely went to centralized platforms that controlled data flow and set the rules. This created a complex dynamic between platforms, users, and regulators. Policymakers struggled to figure out how to regulate the Internet, while participants enjoyed economic benefits but resented the unequal distribution. Meanwhile, platforms felt attacked despite their role in the Internet's expansion. The core issue of Web 2.0 was the concentration of power, influence, data, and capital.

Enter Web 3.0, the third phase of the Internet, which is being powered by blockchain technology. This new era is characterized by decentralization, a growing mistrust of institutions, and a shift in how value is created and captured (Amitabh, 2023a).

In this emerging model, joining a platform does more than grant membership—it transforms participants into co-owners, collectively contributing to the platform's development. The approach fosters a collaborative ecosystem where the success of the platform depends on the shared efforts of its contributors. Although the vision is to scale the platform significantly, initial access is granted selectively to establish a strong, stable foundation.

In this system, creators can secure funding for their projects upfront by engaging directly with those who are interested in their work. These supporters, in turn, receive a stake in the value generated, creating a more defined and mutual relationship between creators and their audience. This structure not only clarifies expectations but also reduces the risks of failure, as the terms are well-established, and the outcomes are concrete. Such models, which emphasize decentralization and collaboration, are becoming central as the Internet shifts into its next phase, where ownership and value creation are more distributed and participatory (Vaughan, 2020).

Network Capital is a peer-to-peer mentorship community that I founded in 2020. It raised capital from Facebook and grew to become one of the world's largest career advancement platforms. My long-term vision for the platform is to make it co-created, co-owned, and co-run by its community members, harnessing the power and benefits of Web 3.0.

Web 3.0 offers a unique opportunity to redefine the role of communities in the economy. With the right structural interventions, platforms, participants, and policymakers, we can make co-owned, co-run, and co-created communities the standard. These communities will be more equitable and egalitarian, with members holding real stakes—equity and the power to influence key decisions. This approach could reshape the dynamics of value creation, where ownership and influence are more widely distributed, aligning with the broader shift to decentralization and shared governance.

7.3 Taylor Swift and the Ownership Controversy

In 2004, at the age of 14, Taylor Swift moved to Nashville to follow her dream of becoming a country pop star. Shortly after, she signed a record deal with Big Machine, a prominent music label. Scott Borchetta, the label's founder, made a bold bet on the unknown singer—a gamble that ultimately generated nearly $300 million. In exchange for a significant cash advance, Swift agreed to give up ownership of the master recordings to her first six albums "in perpetuity"—meaning forever.

At the time, such contracts were standard practice in the music industry, long before streaming services and social media reshaped the business. Artists typically accepted these deals because the costs of recording, distributing, and marketing music were prohibitive, and they often could not afford to cover them on their own. Figures like Borchetta acted as investors, hoping that a few high-risk investments would pay off. Swift was one of his big successes.

Similarly, artists like Prince and George Michael fought against their record labels in court, with varying results. Many remember the iconic image of Prince with the word "slave" written across his cheek. The media had a field day, and public sympathy for the artist was minimal. But in the age of social media, artists now have a direct, unfiltered line to their fans, without needing to rely on traditional media outlets to share their frustrations.

Today, the industry looks drastically different. Swift, along with many other artists, can communicate directly with her audience. This shift is emblematic of the broader changes brought by Web3, which empowers creators to reclaim ownership. Web3 fosters a direct link between creators and consumers, bypassing the old gatekeepers of the industry (DuPont et al., 2024, pp. 1–9).

The evolution of the Internet—Web 1.0, Web 2.0, and now Web 3.0—is crucial for understanding the passion economy. While older millennials have experienced all three phases, Gen Z has grown up in the third, revolutionary phase. The rules of the new digital landscape are still being shaped, as products continue to evolve. Gen Z is not just consuming; they are also creating, investing in, and shaping the future of Web3 platforms. A new era is on the horizon, one that will fundamentally change ownership, creativity, and the way creators interact with their audiences (Amitabh, 2022).

7.4 The Integration of AI in the New Creative Process

When I think of the Internet, I see it as a distribution revolution—a new infrastructure enabling the flow of information and content. Mobile technology amplified this by putting supercomputers in our pockets, dramatically accelerating distribution.

In contrast, generative AI represents a production revolution. While the Internet and mobile's greatest opportunities were centered around distribution—like Google facilitating information sharing or platforms like Facebook, Instagram, and YouTube distributing content—the most exciting potential of generative AI lies in creative tools. Though new networks for distribution will emerge, I'm particularly enthusiastic about products that transform how we create and unlock creativity. Early examples of this shift include ChatGPT and Midjourney, which are paving the way in language and image generation.

The convergence of Web 3.0, AI, and the passion economy marks a transformative shift in how individuals build careers, create value, and interact with technology. Unlike the gig economy's transactional nature, the passion economy thrives on the integration of creativity, ownership, and innovation, giving creators the opportunity to bypass traditional gatekeepers. Web 3.0 is designed to empower individuals by decentralizing ownership and enabling peer-to-peer networks where creators, consumers, and investors co-own and co-create platforms. Generative AI further enhances this ecosystem by democratizing content production, providing accessible creative tools that redefine the boundaries between productivity and artistic expression. Together, these technologies offer unprecedented autonomy, allowing people to monetize their passions while contributing to a more equitable and interconnected economic model.

By 2030, this fusion of technologies has the potential to fundamentally reshape the global digital landscape. As more platforms embrace decentralized governance, young creators, especially Gen Z, are poised to lead the charge, shaping industries through new business models, creative projects, and social innovations. AI will streamline creative workflows, making it possible for more people to pursue their passions full time. Meanwhile, the distributed nature of Web 3.0 will promote greater inclusion by decentralizing access to resources, data, and decision-making. This shift will not only create economic opportunities but also foster more meaningful careers aligned with personal values and societal impact. Ultimately, this new era heralds a more participatory Internet, where communities have real influence, creators own their futures, and technology serves as a catalyst for both individual success and collective progress.

References

Amitabh, U. (2022). *How the passion economy is shaping the future of work.* [online] World Economic Forum. https://www.weforum.org/stories/2022/02/how-the-passion-economy-is-shaping-the-future-of-work/

Amitabh, U. (2023a). *History of the internet and the future of inclusive communities: A case study.* [online] orfonline.org. https://www.orfonline.org/expert-speak/history-of-the-internet-and-the-future-of-inclusive-communities.

Amitabh, U. (2023b). *Passion economy and the side-hustle revolution.* Penguin Random House India Private Limited.

Currier, J. (2021). *The passion economy and the future of work.* NFX. https://www.nfx.com/post/li-jin-passion-attention-economy

DuPont, Q., Kavanagh, D., & Dylan-Ennis, P. (2024). Introduction to Web3: The new cultural economy. In Q. DuPont (Ed.), *Defining Web3: A guide to the new cultural economy* (pp. 1–9). Emerald Publishing.

Polischuk, T., & Gershfeld, A. (2022). *The rise of the passion economy and its impact on the VC market and traditional employment*. European Business Review. https://www.europeanbusinessreview.com/the-rise-of-the-passion-economy-and-its-impact-on-the-vc-market-and-traditional-employment-2/

Vaughan, B. (2020). *The rise of the passion economy—and why you should care*. Forbes. https://www.forbes.com/sites/benjaminvaughan/2020/07/17/the-rise-of-the-passion-economyand-why-you-should-care/

Utkarsh Amitabh A globally recognized entrepreneur, author, and thought leader, Utkarsh is the CEO of Network Capital, a PhD Scholar at Oxford, and a writer at Harvard Business Review. As the founder of one of the world's largest mentorship platforms, he has impacted over 7.5 million students and 150,000 professionals. Armed with degrees in philosophy from the University of Oxford and an MBA from INSEAD, Utkarsh represented the World Economic Forum at Davos. He is the bestselling author of *The Seductive Illusion of Hard Work* (Sage) and *Passion Economy and the Side Hustle Revolution* (Penguin).

Chapter 8
Blockchain Data, Architecture, and Analytics in the Context of Digital Commodities Trading

Oliver Oram

The concept of intelligent commodities emerged from early explorations into how blockchain technology could enhance intelligence and transparency in commodities trading (Boumaiza & Maher, 2024). This vision later evolved into the development of HyYield, reflecting a broader ambition to transform operations across industries such as agriculture, mining, refining, and logistics—sectors traditionally characterized by inefficiencies and financial friction. Contributions from these efforts have informed public discourse, including policy dialogues with the UK Government, international organizations like the OECD and OIV, and media outlets such as the Financial Times.

The initiative began with Chainvine in 2014, focusing on how blockchain could revolutionize digital commodities trading through the creation of verifiable, immutable records. Collaborative work with entities such as the OECD's Reducing Friction in Trade Initiative and the UK Cabinet Office's Ecosystem of Trust laid the groundwork for advancements in interoperability, regulatory compliance, and scalable system architectures (Khawaja & Javidroozi, 2023).

HyYield was established in 2022 in response to the recognition that blockchain alone could not meet the emerging demands of digital commodity ecosystems (Addy et al., 2024). The next evolution required the integration of blockchain with artificial intelligence and advanced analytics. This integration enabled not only transaction tracking but also the enforcement of compliance, automated rule-based trade execution, and greater operational efficiency. Data integrity and automation were identified as key enablers for overcoming longstanding barriers to digital trade, forming the operational foundation of HyYield (Sunmola & Burgess, 2023).

Trust remains a persistent challenge in commodities trading. Legacy systems continue to rely on paper documentation, non-transparent regulatory workflows,

O. Oram (✉)
HyYield Ltd, London, UK
e-mail: oliver@chainvine.com

Y. Xiong (ed.), *Blockchain Analytics for Practitioners*, Business Analytics in Practice, https://doi.org/10.1007/978-3-032-06046-4_8

and intermediaries that introduce delays (Agi & Jha, 2022). Blockchain technologies—demonstrated through Chainvine—offer a transformative alternative by ensuring provenance tracking and creating transparent, tamper-resistant records of commodities' movement from origin to market (Montecchi et al., 2019). These capabilities have been validated through real-world deployments, including agricultural supply chains and international trade contexts.

As development progressed under the HyYield initiative, it became increasingly evident that the core strength of blockchain lies in its capacity to integrate with AI-driven analytics. The concept of intelligent commodities extends beyond transactional tracking; it demands predictive capabilities and autonomous decision-making (Hussain & Al-Turjman, 2021). Artificial intelligence enables the analysis of large volumes of blockchain data to enforce structured trading rules, detect fraudulent activity, and enhance compliance monitoring (Seo & Huh, 2024). This shift—highlighted in public commentary including interviews with outlets such as the Financial Times—underscores how advanced analytics can mitigate market manipulation and foster more efficient trading ecosystems.

Interoperability has also emerged as a central focus. Chainvine's blockchain sandbox collaboration with K&L Gates explored the role of smart contracts in automating trade execution and verifying regulatory compliance (Dütsch & Steinecke, 2019; Boumaiza & Maher, 2024). A key technical challenge has been ensuring seamless operation across diverse blockchain networks, including Ethereum, Hyperledger, and other emerging frameworks (Durfee et al., 2025). In this context, standardization efforts led by organizations such as the OECD and ISO have proven essential in aligning blockchain-based compliance infrastructures with traditional financial systems (Jia et al., 2023).

At HyYield, further progress has been achieved by embedding AI-driven automation into rule enforcement mechanisms. The platform's innovation centers on ensuring that digital trading activity adheres to predefined regulatory rulebooks, with AI ensuring real-time validation and exception handling. Recognizing the sensitivity of data in regulated environments, privacy-preserving techniques such as zero-knowledge proofs and differential privacy have been examined as tools for achieving a balance between transparency and data protection—an increasingly vital requirement in digital commodities ecosystems (Liu, 2022; Lavin et al., 2024).

This trajectory—from early blockchain experiments in provenance validation to fully automated, AI-enhanced compliance systems—marks a pivotal evolution in the role of decentralized technologies. Blockchain is no longer confined to record-keeping but is now foundational to rule enforcement, risk mitigation, and real-time regulatory oversight at scale (Ressi et al., 2024).

Beyond the commodities sector, Chainvine's research and partnerships have intersected with broader themes of financial inclusion and sustainability. Contributions to initiatives under the Commonwealth Partnership for Technology Management (CPTM) have emphasized the role of emerging technologies in accelerating commercial efficiency while advancing ethical and socially responsible practices (Baker et al., 2022). These efforts are aligned with the United Nations Sustainable Development Goals (SDGs), particularly in domains such as environmental stewardship and ethical sourcing (Mulligan et al., 2024). One notable application includes the use of blockchain to certify geographical origin—for example, verifying that fish exported from the Seychelles are sustainably sourced, thereby supporting traceability, biodiversity protection, and the reduction of illegal fishing practices (Ismail et al., 2023).

The concept of a National Asset Management System has been explored as a means to add value by integrating blockchain, artificial intelligence, and machine learning for the authentication and management of national assets (Wang et al., 2022; Shafik, 2025). This approach holds significant potential to transform how countries govern and monetize their resources, promoting transparency, traceability, and long-term economic benefit (Ainur et al., 2024). A key illustration of this potential is seen in the Seychelles–CPTM–Chainvine initiative, which digitally certifies Seychellois tuna to assure ethical sourcing and environmental accountability.

This vision is grounded in the recognition that technological advancement is inseparable from institutional process. Effective implementation of innovation is less a matter of the underlying technology itself and more about how it is embedded into existing structures. As often emphasized in digital transformation discourse, success is "80% process and 20% technology." Cisco has projected that approximately 10% of global GDP will be stored on blockchain infrastructure by 2027—an estimate that underscores the urgency and relevance of distributed ledger technologies (DLTs) for national development strategies (Slagell et al., 2004; Helebrandt et al., 2018). Importantly, such applications need not involve volatile cryptocurrencies; rather, they can focus on the secure management of public assets, creation of national data ecosystems, and governance enhancements aligned with the Sustainable Development Goals (SDGs) (Kalaiarasi & Kirubahari, 2023).

This framework reflects a broader strategy aimed at advancing financial inclusion, operational efficiency, and transparency in global commodities trading. By adopting intelligent, data-driven technologies, national and international actors are better positioned to participate in a next-generation digital economy characterized by automation, verifiability, and optimized decision-making (Ressi et al., 2024). While the application of blockchain in commodities trading is still unfolding, current developments in AI integration, interoperability, and regulatory alignment suggest that foundational shifts are well underway. What was once a theoretical model for "intelligent commodities" is now evolving into a new standard—one that redefines the future of trade in the digital era.

References

Addy, W. A., et al. (2024). Algorithmic trading and AI: A review of strategies and market impact. *World Journal of Advanced Engineering Technology and Sciences, 11*(1), 258–267.

Agi, M. A. N., & Jha, A. K. (2022). Blockchain technology in the supply chain: An integrated theoretical perspective of organizational adoption. *International Journal of Production Economics, 247*, 108458. https://doi.org/10.1016/j.ijpe.2022.108458

Ainur, J., et al. (2024). Analysis of research on the implementation of Blockchain technologies in regional electoral processes. *International Journal of Electrical and Computer Engineering, 14*(3), 2854–2867.

Baker, P., Breitsprecher, M., & Guthoff, D.M. (2022) '*Blockchain and financing for sustainable development: Foresight study*. [online] BMZ Digital. Global'. Deutsche Gesellschaft für Internationale Zusammenarbeit (GIZ) GmbH.

Boumaiza, A., & Maher, K. (2024). Leveraging blockchain technology to enhance transparency and efficiency in carbon trading markets. *International Journal of Electrical Power & Energy Systems, 162*, 110225. https://doi.org/10.1016/j.ijepes.2024.110225

Durfee, J., et al. (2025). Interoperability of blockchain systems and the future of payments. *Liberty Street Economics* [Preprint]. Retrieved April 4, 2025, from https://papers.ssrn.com/sol3/papers.cfm?abstract_id=5196482

Dütsch, G., & Steinecke, N. (2019). *Use cases for blockchain technology in energy & commodity trading, 2017, PWC Dostupno na: https://www.pwc.com/gx/en/industries/assets/blockchain--technology-inenergy.pdfDatumpristupa*, 1.

Helebrandt, P., et al. (2018). Blockchain adoption for monitoring and management of enterprise networks. In *2018 IEEE 9th annual information technology, Electronics and Mobile Communication Conference (IEMCON)* (pp. 1221–1225). IEEE. Retrieved April 4, 2025, from https://ieeexplore.ieee.org/abstract/document/8614960/

Hussain, A. A., & Al-Turjman, F. (2021). Artificial intelligence and blockchain: A review. *Transactions on Emerging Telecommunications Technologies, 32*(9), e4268. https://doi.org/10.1002/ett.4268

Ismail, S., et al. (2023). Toward an intelligent blockchain ioT-enabled fish supply chain: A review and conceptual framework. *Sensors, 23*(11), 5136.

Jia, X., et al. (2023). 'International standardization of blockchain and distributed ledger technology: Overlaps, gaps and challenges.', *CMES-Computer Modeling in Engineering & Sciences, 137*(2). Retrieved April 4, 2025, from https://search.ebscohost.com/login.aspx?direct=true&profile=ehost&scope=site&authtype=crawler&jrnl=15261492&AN=164664311&h=rYivhY2y88BkWZuMHcCxOiAS9ZPHwAAnUahjiUi8eLTJRJSEMMa1ndHVxd2AmtoBJCBjfZoElzyCyzPUwDiycw%3D%3D&crl=c

Kalaiarasi, H., & Kirubahari, S. (2023) Green finance for sustainable development using blockchain technology. In *Green blockchain technology for sustainable smart cities* (pp. 167–185). Elsevier. Retrieved April 4, 2025, from https://www.sciencedirect.com/science/article/pii/B9780323954075000037

Khawaja, S., & Javidroozi, V. (2023). Blockchain technology as an enabler for cross-sectoral systems integration for developing smart sustainable cities. *IET Smart Cities, 5*(3), 151–172. https://doi.org/10.1049/smc2.12059

Lavin, R., et al. (2024). *A survey on the applications of zero-knowledge proofs*. arXiv. https://doi.org/10.48550/arXiv.2408.00243.

Liu, S. (2022) Privacy protection revolution: Zero-knowledge proof, in *2022 International Conference on Data Analytics, Computing and Artificial Intelligence (ICDACAI)* (pp. 394–397). IEEE. Retrieved April 4, 2025, from https://ieeexplore.ieee.org/abstract/document/9973872/?casa_token=ormlKXBkhkwAAAAA:3Uf3ElC2FpeM5RsxI1HVHdfzT-WoWToo937cbMWsR21DfL1Oqc-LrbXk50Pr1d4jHJr3tdmLZA

Montecchi, M., Plangger, K., & Etter, M. (2019). It's real, trust me! Establishing supply chain provenance using blockchain. *Business Horizons, 62*(3), 283–293. https://doi.org/10.1016/j.bushor.2019.01.008

Mulligan, C., Morsfield, S., & Cheikosman, E. (2024). Blockchain for sustainability: A systematic literature review for policy impact. *Telecommunications Policy, 48*(2), 102676. https://doi.org/10.1016/j.telpol.2023.102676

Ressi, D., et al. (2024). AI-enhanced blockchain technology: A review of advancements and opportunities. *Journal of Network and Computer Applications, 225*, 103858. https://doi.org/10.1016/j.jnca.2024.103858

Seo, Y.-S., & Huh, J.-H. (2024). Artificial intelligence in finance: Coffee commodity trading big data for informed decision making, *IEEE Access* [Preprint]. Retrieved April 4, 2025, from https://ieeexplore.ieee.org/abstract/document/10549867/

Shafik, W. (2025). Integrating emerging technologies for digital asset management. In *Intelligent data-driven techniques for security of digital assets* (pp. 1–19). CRC Press, Taylor & Francis.

Slagell, A., Wang, J., & Yurcik, W. (2004) Network log anonymization: Application of crypto-pan to cisco netflows. In *Proceedings of the Workshop on Secure Knowledge Management 2004*. Citeseer. Retrieved April 4, 2025, from https://citeseerx.ist.psu.edu/document?repid=rep1&type=pdf&doi=accc29066bb4eb5d0f4dc71e75ef4a585015055a

Sunmola, F., & Burgess, P. (2023). Transparency by design for blockchain-based supply chains. *Procedia Computer Science, 217*, 1256–1265. https://doi.org/10.1016/j.procs.2022.12.324

Wang, Z., et al. (2022). Business innovation based on artificial intelligence and Blockchain technology. *Information Processing & Management, 59*(1), 102759.

Oliver Oram is the Founder and CEO of HyYield, a digital platform revolutionizing critical commodity trading by embedding geopolitical risk into smarter, more transparent markets. He previously founded Chainvine, a Blockchain/DLT enterprise platform, where he pioneered one of the first Digital Product Passports, enhancing supply chain transparency and aligning operations with SDGs, ESG goals, and green finance. Oliver has advised Commonwealth central bank governors on blockchain and digital assets and brings deep expertise from the financial technology sector. His work spans technology, sustainability, and global trade, positioning him as a leading voice in the future of sustainable digital economies.

Chapter 9
Conclusions

Amit Kumar Jaiswal and Tao Tang

Blockchain technology has emerged as a revolutionary force, fundamentally reshaping how digital transactions and records are managed (Tripathi et al., 2023). From its inception with Bitcoin as a decentralized digital currency to its evolution into a sophisticated ecosystem powering decentralized finance (DeFi), supply chain management, healthcare, and beyond, blockchain continues to redefine traditional paradigms of trust, transparency, and data integrity (Ortu et al., 2024).

The foundational principles of decentralization, immutability, and peer-to-peer networking, emphasized throughout this book, have proven essential in harnessing blockchain's transformative capabilities (Mafrur, 2025). Decentralization, in particular, has established itself as a cornerstone by distributing control across multiple participants, significantly enhancing security, transparency, and resilience (Kuznetsov et al., 2024). Meanwhile, various consensus mechanisms, such as Proof of Work (PoW) and Proof of Stake (PoS), have enabled blockchain networks to achieve and maintain collective agreement without central authority, reinforcing both security and efficiency.

Blockchain's technological evolution from the foundational developments of Bitcoin to Ethereum's smart contract capabilities has been marked by continuous innovation (Polge et al., 2021). Ethereum transformed blockchain into a programmable environment supporting decentralized applications (DApps), paving the way

A. K. Jaiswal (✉)
Endless Protocol, Guildford, UK

University of Surrey, Guildford, UK

Indian Institute of Technology (BHU) Varanasi, Varanasi, India
e-mail: amit@endless.link; a.jaiswal@surrey.ac.uk; amit.chr@iitbhu.ac.in

T. Tang
Surrey Academy for Blockchain and Metaverse Applications, Surrey Business School, University of Surrey, Guildford, UK
e-mail: t.tang@surrey.ac.uk

Y. Xiong (ed.), *Blockchain Analytics for Practitioners*, Business Analytics in Practice, https://doi.org/10.1007/978-3-032-06046-4_9

for entirely new economic interactions. However, challenges such as scalability, high transaction costs, and security vulnerabilities in second-generation blockchains have stimulated ongoing research and innovation, leading to the rise of third-generation blockchains like Polkadot, Cardano, and Cosmos (Allen, 2024). These newer platforms have prioritized scalability, interoperability, and sustainability, addressing critical limitations and integrating blockchain more seamlessly with emerging technologies, including Artificial Intelligence (AI) and the Internet of Things (IoT).

The growth of blockchain has given rise to the critical field of blockchain analytics (Bartoletti et al., 2017; Dillenberger et al., 2019). Positioned uniquely at the intersection of cryptography, economics, and data science, blockchain analytics provides invaluable insights by leveraging blockchain's inherent transparency and immutability. Distinct from traditional analytics, it deals with unique technical challenges such as managing vast transaction volumes, addressing pseudonymous user identities, and interpreting immutable datasets. Through various analytical layers from simple wallet interactions to complex smart contract executions blockchain analytics has significantly impacted financial services, supply chains, decentralized finance, and NFT markets. Its importance in strategic business decision-making, regulatory compliance, and fraud detection underscores its central role in blockchain's future trajectory.

Delving deeper into blockchain's architecture and operational mechanisms further reveals the critical role of cryptography in securing blockchain systems (Biais et al., 2023). Cryptographic hash functions, hash chains, Merkle trees, and digital signatures have collectively ensured data integrity and enabled secure, transparent, and efficient transaction validation processes. Blockchain's decentralized ledger technology, consensus algorithms, and peer-to-peer architecture ensure the immutability and resilience of blockchain networks. Understanding these elements has proven fundamental for leveraging blockchain analytics effectively, enabling more precise interpretations and predictions about network behavior and participant interactions.

Practically, blockchain's unique attributes have found substantial application within modern business ecosystems (Beck et al., 2017). Initially constrained by regulatory concerns surrounding public blockchain anonymity, enterprises have increasingly embraced permissioned blockchain models. Platforms like Hyperledger Fabric and R3 Corda illustrate how blockchain's transparency and immutability can be tailored to regulated environments, significantly reducing fraud risks in areas such as trade finance and supply chain logistics. Moreover, blockchain-based synchronization across multiple enterprises offers unparalleled efficiency in data verification, compliance, and auditability, creating new competitive advantages and collaborative opportunities across industries. The emergence of central bank digital currencies (CBDCs) further exemplifies blockchain's expansive potential within monetary policy and financial stability frameworks.

However, the expansion of blockchain use cases also brought specific challenges to the forefront (Viriyasitavat et al., 2019). Sybil attacks, particularly within the Web3 ecosystem, illustrate critical vulnerabilities that blockchain projects must address. Malicious actors have exploited token airdrops through multiple wallet creations, necessitating robust detection methods. Analytical techniques, such as network analysis and behavioral clustering algorithms, combined with non-analytical methods like Know-Your-Customer (KYC) and proof-of-humanity protocols, have emerged as essential strategies to mitigate such vulnerabilities. The nuanced balance between security and user accessibility highlighted through practical case studies underscores the importance of sophisticated, integrated frameworks that prioritize fairness, security, and sustainable economic participation in blockchain networks.

Another critical challenge in blockchain's evolving landscape is the regulatory complexity surrounding decentralized finance (DeFi). Operating in a decentralized, permissionless environment, DeFi challenges traditional regulatory frameworks designed for centralized intermediaries (Ozili, 2022; Auer et al., 2024). Regulators globally face unprecedented challenges in enforcing compliance, managing pseudonymity-related risks, and navigating cross-border regulatory arbitrage (Schär, 2021). Moreover, ambiguous asset classifications and varying national regulatory standards complicate regulatory efforts further, highlighting the necessity for flexible, technology-neutral approaches complemented by targeted blockchain-specific regulation (Gudgeon et al., 2020). International regulatory collaboration, coupled with deeper technical understanding and proactive industry self-regulation, will be crucial in fostering an innovative yet secure DeFi environment.

Looking forward, the integration of blockchain with emerging digital paradigms, such as Web 3.0 and generative AI, promises even more transformative possibilities. The rise of Web 3.0, a decentralized, user-owned, and co-created Internet is closely intertwined with blockchain's decentralization principles (Mohit, 2022). By empowering users through greater ownership, direct monetization of passions, and peer-driven governance, Web 3.0 significantly disrupts traditional economic and creative models. Generative AI further amplifies this shift by democratizing creativity and productivity, enabling individuals to engage meaningfully in the passion economy (Korinek, 2023). The convergence of these technologies signals a profound realignment of digital economic structures, promising greater autonomy, equity, and innovative potential for creators and communities worldwide.

Ultimately, blockchain's transformative journey underscores its remarkable adaptability and resilience in addressing complex technological, economic, and social challenges (Casino et al., 2019). While significant barriers such as scalability, regulatory uncertainty, privacy concerns, and security vulnerabilities remain, continuous innovation and collaboration within the blockchain community hold immense promise for overcoming these obstacles (Shukla et al., 2024). Blockchain analytics, robust cryptographic foundations, permissioned networks, Sybil attack mitigations, flexible regulatory frameworks, and decentralized, user-centric Web3 ecosystems are essential components that will define blockchain's future trajectory (Biais et al., 2023).

As blockchain technology matures, its influence will undoubtedly grow, reshaping industries and societal structures globally. Continued dialogue among technologists, policymakers, researchers, businesses, and users remains vital in guiding blockchain toward its fullest potential, creating an equitable, transparent, and resilient digital future.

References

Allen, D. W. E. (2024). Crypto airdrops: An evolutionary approach. *Journal of Evolutionary Economics, 34*(4), 849–872. https://doi.org/10.1007/s00191-024-00874-6

Auer, R., et al. (2024). The technology of decentralized finance (DeFi). *Digital Finance, 6*(1), 55–95. https://doi.org/10.1007/s42521-023-00088-8

Bartoletti, M., et al. (2017). A general framework for blockchain analytics. In *Proceedings of the 1st workshop on scalable and resilient infrastructures for distributed ledgers* (pp. 1–6). Association for Computing Machinery (SERIAL'17). https://doi.org/10.1145/3152824.3152831

Beck, R., et al. (2017). Blockchain technology in business and information systems research. *Business & Information Systems Engineering, 59*(6), 381–384. https://doi.org/10.1007/s12599-017-0505-1

Biais, B., et al. (2023). Advances in Blockchain and crypto economics. *Management Science, 69*(11), 6417–6426. https://doi.org/10.1287/mnsc.2023.intro.v69.n11

Casino, F., Dasaklis, T. K., & Patsakis, C. (2019). A systematic literature review of blockchain-based applications: Current status, classification and open issues. *Telematics and Informatics, 36*, 55–81. https://doi.org/10.1016/j.tele.2018.11.006

Dillenberger, D. N., et al. (2019). Blockchain analytics and artificial intelligence. *IBM Journal of Research and Development, 63*(2/3), 5:1–5:14. https://doi.org/10.1147/JRD.2019.2900638

Gudgeon, L., et al. (2020). The decentralized financial crisis. In *2020 Crypto Valley Conference on Blockchain Technology (CVCBT)* (pp. 1–15). https://doi.org/10.1109/CVCBT50464.2020.00005

Korinek, A. (2023). Generative AI for economic research: Use cases and implications for economists. *Journal of Economic Literature, 61*(4), 1281–1317. https://doi.org/10.1257/jel.20231736

Kuznetsov, O., et al. (2024). Merkle trees in blockchain: A study of collision probability and security implications. *Internet of Things, 26*, 101193. Available at:. https://doi.org/10.1016/j.iot.2024.101193

Mafrur, R. (2025). Blockchain Data Analytics: Review and Challenges. arXiv. https://doi.org/10.48550/arXiv.2503.09165

Mohit, M. (2022). The Metaverse and Web3: A new era of decentralized digital ecosystems. *International Journal of Innovative Research in Computer and Communication Engineering, 10*(6), 4771–4778.

Ortu, M., et al. (2024). Taxonomic insights into ethereum smart contracts by linking application categories to security vulnerabilities. *Scientific Reports, 14*(1), 23433. https://doi.org/10.1038/s41598-024-73454-0

Ozili, P. K. (2022). Decentralized finance research and developments around the world. *Journal of Banking and Financial Technology, 6*(2), 117–133. https://doi.org/10.1007/s42786-022-00044-x

Polge, J., Robert, J., & Le Traon, Y. (2021). Permissioned blockchain frameworks in the industry: A comparison. *ICT Express, 7*(2), 229–233. https://doi.org/10.1016/j.icte.2020.09.002

Schär, F. (2021). Decentralized finance: On Blockchain and smart contract-based financial markets. *Review of the Federal Reserve Bank of St Louis, 103*(2), 153–174. https://doi.org/10.20955/r.103.153-74

Shukla, A., et al. (2024). An overview of blockchain research and future agenda: Insights from structural topic modeling. *Journal of Innovation & Knowledge, 9*(4), 100605. Available at:. https://doi.org/10.1016/j.jik.2024.100605

Tripathi, G., Ahad, M. A., & Casalino, G. (2023). A comprehensive review of blockchain technology: Underlying principles and historical background with future challenges. *Decision Analytics Journal, 9*, 100344. https://doi.org/10.1016/j.dajour.2023.100344

Viriyasitavat, W., Anuphaptrirong, T., & Hoonsopon, D. (2019). When blockchain meets internet of things: Characteristics, challenges, and business opportunities. *Journal of Industrial Information Integration, 15*, 21–28. https://doi.org/10.1016/j.jii.2019.05.002

MIX
Papier aus verantwortungsvollen Quellen
Paper from responsible sources
FSC® C105338

If you have any concerns about our products,
you can contact us on
ProductSafety@springernature.com

In case Publisher is established outside the EU,
the EU authorized representative is:
Springer Nature Customer Service Center GmbH
Europaplatz 3, 69115 Heidelberg, Germany

Printed by Libri Plureos GmbH
in Hamburg, Germany